William Curtis

A Short History and Description of the Town of Alton

In the County of Southampton

William Curtis

A Short History and Description of the Town of Alton
In the County of Southampton

ISBN/EAN: 9783337005054

Printed in Europe, USA, Canada, Australia, Japan

Cover: Foto ©ninafisch / pixelio.de

More available books at **www.hansebooks.com**

Plate I.

A SHORT

HISTORY AND DESCRIPTION

OF

The Town of Alton

IN THE COUNTY OF SOUTHAMPTON.

COMPILED BY

WILLIAM CURTIS, M.R.C.S., L.S.A.

Winchester:
WARREN & SON, PRINTERS & PUBLISHERS.

London:
SIMPKIN & CO., LIMITED, STATIONERS' HALL COURT, E.C.

—

1896.

PREFACE.

THE present work is largely the outcome of an attempt to write a short history and description of Alton for the Mechanics Institution, but I soon found that the materials began to accumulate, and proved so numerous, that I ventured to bring them together in book form.

Only one small sketch of Alton has appeared in print before, so far as I am aware, and that was written by Mr. Hy. Smith, and published in the Town in the year 1873.

My information has been obtained from very varied sources, from the British Museum, Record Office, and Lambeth Palace Library, from many Authors, amongst whom may be mentioned, T. G. Shore, Esq., Rev. G. N. Godwin, The Hampshire Record Society's Publications, the Church and Parish Books and Registers, etc.

Many friends have also rendered me most kind and valuable assistance, for which I beg to tender them my most grateful thanks ; amongst whom I should like to mention the Rev. T. Hervey, Colmer ; Rev. F. Whyley, Alton ; Rev. J. Vaughan, Portchester, Rev. H. E. Victor, Brighton ; Frederick Crowley, Esq., Ashdell, Alton ; and Benjamin Winstone, Esq., Ockeridge, Epping ; and many others too numerous to mention.

My best thanks are due to Mr. Piggott for the able assistance he so kindly rendered me, in reading through the manuscript before putting it into the hands of the Publishers.

I also beg to thank Mr. Wm. Curtis Green for his beautiful Pen and Ink Sketches of the Parish Church of St. Lawrence and of the old Norman Arches ; Mr. Close, for his two excellent Wood Engravings of Vicarage Hill and Tanhouse Lane ; and Messrs. Vaus and Crampton, of the Helios Works, Alton and London, for their excellent illustrations.

To Messrs. Warren and Son I wish to express my appreciation of the kind interest they have taken in the work, and the care and skilful workmanship exhibited in the printing and publishing of the Book.

As this is my first attempt as an Author, I trust I shall obtain the indulgence of my readers for any imperfections in my work, and in offering it to the Inhabitants of my native Town, I do so with the hope that they may be as interested in reading it as I have been in compiling it.

WILLIAM CURTIS.

Alton,
    December, 1896.

CONTENTS.

LIST OF ILLUSTRATIONS.

ERRATA.

Page 58—first line, last paragraph, for "west" *read* "south" entrance.

,, 79—third line, second paragraph, for "succeeding" *read* "preceding."

,, 113—first side note, for "Cemetery opened, 1895," *read* "Cemetery opened, 1856."

CHRONOLOGICAL SUMMARY.

A.D.

600. Alton probably amongst the earliest West Saxon Townships.

825. Grant by King Egbert, of land at Alton to Monastery of St. Peter and St. Paul, Winchester.

901. King Alfred left land at Alton to his eldest son.

980. A battle fought at Alton in the last Danish Invasion.

1001. A sanguinary battle fought between the Saxons and Danes.

1041. In King Edward the Confessor's time, Alton a royal manor.

1041. The Abbot of St. Peter's de Wincester holds Aultone.

1066. Half Alton, with its Church, etc., given by King William to Hyde Abbey.

1066. Alton required to furnish men for army at Hastings.

1084. Hyde Abbey held Aultone.

1087. Grant of Alton Church by King William to Abbot of New Minster.

1087. Grant of Alton by Rinuallo, Abbot of New Minster.

1101. Battle on verge of being fought and treaty signed between Henry I and his Brother Robert.

1124. Alton Church restored to the Blessed Peter, Prior Ingulf and his monks.

1135. King Stephen gave Neatham and Church to the Monks at Waverley.

1174. The Canterbury Pilgrims.

1204. King John at Alton.

1207 to 1546. Land Holders.

1216. Alton governed by Bailiffs and Burgesses.

1217. King John at Alton.

1250. Permission given to celebrate divine service in Oratory at Neteham.

1262 to 1361. Chancery Inquisitions, etc.

1267. Adam Gurdon the Outlaw.

1272. Sir Adam made Warden.

1290 to 1315. Patent Rolls.

1295. Hampshire first represented in Parliament.

1307. Edward II granted a Fair at Alton.

A.D.

1307. William de Alton, a Dominican Friar, an Author, born at Alton.

1482. Lands bought in Town and Neighbourhood, by Winchester College.

1490. View of Frank-pledge.

1510 to 1535. Grants.

1535. The Rectory of Alton appropriated to Hyde Abbey.

1560. John Pitts, or Friar Pitts, an Author, born in Alton.

1560. Security for Change of Residence.

1580 to 1644. State Papers.

1615. The Parish Registers commence.

1625. Churchwardens' Accounts begin.

1635. King Charles I came through the Town.

1641. Eggar's Grammar School founded.

1642. Civil War.

1643. Dec. 1. Lord Crawford occupied Alton with his Army.

1643. Dec. 13. The great battle in the Church.

1649. Survey of Church Lands.

1653. Geales Almshouses built.

1665. The Plague.

1666. Alton Tokens.

1666. The date of Old Map of Alton.

1669. King Charles II passed through the Town.

1672. Society of Friends' Meeting house built.

1684. King James II rode through the Town.

1696. Congregational Chapel built.

1742. New Treble Bell added to Belfry.

1746. William Curtis, Botanist, born in Alton.

1750. The Alton Machine or Coach.

1785. The six old bells recast and two new bells added.

1792. Union Workhouse erected.

1803. The first Volunteers in Napoleon's time.

1812. Town Hall built.

1814. French Prisoners located in Alton.

1815. Appropriation of Church Seats.

1815. Public dinner when peace was proclaimed.

1819. London and Gosport Road made by Macadam.

1825. Hampshire Friendly Society started.

1829. New Barrel Organ erected in Church.

1830. Riots threatened.

1831. A Board of Health appointed.

A.D.

1834. Boundaries of Parish perambulated.
1837. Mechanics' Institution founded.
1838. Queen's Coronation. Public dinner.
1839. Frescoe Paintings discovered in Church.
1840. Town Hall enlarged.
1841. National Schools erected.
1843. British Schools started.
1844. Gas Works constructed.
1844. Independent Order of Oddfellows started.
1845. Police Station built.
1846. Wesleyan Chapel built.
1850. An additional Service in Church added on Sunday evenings.
1852. London and South Western Railway opened.
1855. Mechanics' Institution occupied their new premises in Market Street.
1856. Cemetery opened.
1856. Burial Board formed.
1856. The old Churchyard closed.
1856. Museum opened.
1858. Presentation of Plate to William Curtis, President of the Mechanics' Institution.
1860. Treading the boundaries of the Parish.
1860. Local Board formed.
1860. Volunteer Rifle Corps gazetted.
1862. The Sewerage Works first constructed.
1863. Prince and Princess of Wales' wedding celebrated.
1863. Volunteer Fire Brigade formed.
1865. Alton and Winchester Railway opened.
1866. Treading Bounds given up.
1867. The Church restored.
1867. New Organ erected.
1867. Church Rates discontinued.
1867. New British Schools built.
1867. Town Footpaths re-paved with Brick.
1868. Office of Sidesmen revived.
1868. Cottage Hospital established.
1869. Churchwardens' Staffs of Office presented to Church.
1869. Ancient Order of Foresters started.
1869. Normandy Cottage opened for six old women.
1872. Constables given up for Police.

A.D.

1873. Church Spire restored and covered with oak shingle.
1874. All Saints' Church consecrated.
1876. Water Works started.
1878, Charities of the Parish, Report on.
1880. Church Spire struck by lightning.
1880. The new Cottage Hospital opened.
1880. The Assembly Rooms opened.
1880. The new Mechanics Institution and Museum opened.
1880. The Museum presented to the Institution by
         Wm. Curtis, Esq.
1881. The Museum to be named " The Curtis Museum," after
         the late President.
1881. Additional land taken into Cemetery and consecrated.
1886. New Oak Choir Stalls added to Church.
1889. Bells rehung and No. 7 recast.
1889. A new Clock added to Church Tower with Westminster
         Chimes.
1890. Post Office removed to its present large premises.
1890. Recreation Ground opened.
1891. Baptist Chapel built.
1891. Salvation Army Barracks built.
1893. Purchase of Normandy House and Garden for Mechanics'
         Institution Extension.
1893. The old building adapted for Museum, and Art and
         Technical Schools.
1893. Constitutional Club opened.
1893. Infectious Hospital opened.
1895. Church Lads' Brigade started.
1895. The Order of St. Paul settled at Beach Camp.
1896. Additional Land bought to enlarge Cemetery.

History of Alton.

IN writing this sketch of Alton, it is intended to trace its history as far as possible from the earliest ages to the present time. Material for this purpose is very meagre, but within the last few years a great deal has been done to bring to light the hidden things of the past.

The town of Alton stands in the north-eastern portion of the County, and is now placed in the Eastern, or Petersfield, Parliamentary Division. It is situated in a purely agricultural district, is 47 miles distant from London, 12 from Aldershot, 9 from Farnham, 18 from Winchester, 30 from Southampton and Portsmouth, 12 from Petersfield, 11 from Basingstoke, and 8 from Odiham.

Alton is divided into five Manors :—

> The Manor of Alton Eastbrook.
> The Manor of Alton Westbrook.
> The Manor of Chauntsingers.
> The Manor of Truncheaunts.
> The Manor of Anstey.

Taking the origin of the name itself, there have been two opinions with regard to it. The older and more commonly received derivation is from the Anglo-Saxon, *eald*, old, and *tun*, a town ; or simply old town.

Origin of the Name.

But in Lewis' *Topographical Dictionary* it states that "Al" in Alton, or Aulton in Hants, is not, as has been assumed, the old town, but the town on the "Awel," the name of the river, or as Kemble says, "of the head springs of a river."

Woodward and Wilks' *History* speaks of Alton as the "town of the stream," not as misreading of its ancient name has interpreted it, "the ancient town."[1]

[1] Woodward and Wilks' *History of Hampshire*, Vol. iii, p. 308.

B

In *Memorials of a Quiet Life*, by Augustus Hare, it says, Saxon, *ea-wal-ton*, "the place of beautiful springs," corrupted to Awltoun (Domesday Book), hence Alton.

It was formerly spelt in a variety of ways; Aulton, Aultone, Altone, Aweltone, and Æweltune.

In early days it was no doubt a very small place, and of minor importance to Neatham in King Alfred's time, as Alton was in the Hundred of Neatham.

Population.

On reference to the old map of Alton, dated 1666, we find about 225 houses represented, and on taking an average of five persons to a house, it would bring the population at that time, roughly speaking, to 1125.

The population of Alton Parish, according to the official returns since 1801, was as follows :—

Date		Population		Increase in 10 years		Increase since 1801
1801	...	2026	...	——	...	——
1811	...	2316	...	290	...	290
1821	...	2499	...	183	...	473
1831	...	2742	...	243	...	716
1841	...	3139	...	397	...	1113
1851	...	3538	...	399	...	1512
1861	...	3769	...	231	...	1743
1871	...	4092	...	323	...	2066
1881	...	4497	...	405	...	2471
1891	...	4671	...	174	...	2645

Acreage.

The area in acres in the Urban District is 3925.

Rateable Value.

The rateable value, £20,537.

Polling Districts.

POLLING DISTRICTS.

Parishes comprised in the Eastern or Petersfield Division of Hants, and showing to which Polling District they belong. These are arranged in accordance with the " Redistribution of Seats Bill " of 1885 :—

Polling District.			Parishes.
Alton	...		Alton, East Worldham, Holybourne, Neatham, Shalden, West Worldham.
Bentley	...	...	Bentley, Coldrey, Froyle.
Bentworth	...	...	Bentworth, Lasham.
Binsted	...	...	Binsted, Kingsley.

Plate II.

THE HUNDREDS OF HANTSHIRE.—1600.

Polling District.		Parishes.
Bishop's Waltham	...	Bishop's Waltham.
Bramshott ...	...	Bramshott.
Brown Candover	...	Brown Candover, Chilton Candover, Northington, Swarraton.
Catherington	...	Blendworth, Catherington, Clanfield.
Chawton ...	...	Chawton, Farringdon.
Curdridge ...	...	Curdridge.
Dockenfield	...	Dockenfield.
Droxford ...	...	Droxford, Soberton (part of), Swanmore.
Eastmeon ...	...	Eastmeon.
East Tisted...	...	Colemore, East Tisted, Newton Valence (part of), Priors Dean.
Froxfield ...	...	Froxfield, Privett.
Hambledon ...	...	Hambledon.
Headley ...	...	Headley.
Hinton Ampner	...	Beauworth, Bramdean, Cheriton, Hinton Ampner, Kilmiston.
Idsworth ...	...	Chalton, Idsworth.
Langrish ...	...	Langrish.
Liss ...	...	Greatham, Hawkley, Liss.
Medstead ...	...	Medstead, Wield.
Meonstoke ...	...	Corhampton, Exton, Meonstoke.
New Alresford	...	Bighton, Bishop's Sutton, Godsfield, Itchen Stoke, New Alresford, Old Alresford, Ovington, Tichborne.
Newtown ...	...	Soberton (part of).
Petersfield ...	...	Buriton, Petersfield, Sheet, Steep.
Ropley ...	...	Ropley, West Tisted.
Selborne ...	...	Empshott, Hartley Mauditt, Newton Valence (part of), Selborne.
Shedfield ...	...	Shedfield.
Upham ...	...	Durley, Upham.
Westmeon ...	...	Warnford, Westmeon.

8550 electors, 1895.

ANCIENT HISTORY.

" The earliest inhabitants we can trace in this part of England are those who made rude stone implements by chipping flints into the form of hatchets, spear heads, and other weapons, and are known as the Paleolithic people, or men of the early stone age. They have also been named the River Drift men, from the circumstance that these relics are found in beds of gravel, which have been formed

Paleolithic period.

by the drifting power of rivers and floods, that have washed the gravel down from higher parts of the country." [1]

Flint celts.

A few of these flint celts, or axes, have been found at Alton, Milcourt, Kingsley, East and West Worldham, and Newton Common, specimens of which are exhibited in the Curtis Museum.

" The Paleolithic period is so remote from our own that England at that time was no doubt connected with the Continent."

Neolithic period.

" The bones of the people of the Neolithic, or Newer Stone Age, are the earliest human remains which are found in Hampshire or the adjacent counties, and they have been found in barrows or tumuli." [1]

Celts.

The precise settlement of the Celts in Hampshire is unknown. " The Celtic earthworks were the refuges which the tribes or clans threw up as defences primarily against the attacks of neighbouring tribes. In Hampshire these several tribal clans were in some cases separated by wide belts of forest land. The forest land south of Alton, which formed the western extremity of the great forest after-

Andredsweald.

wards known as the Andredsweald, cut off the Celtic people living in the valley of the Wey from those living in the valleys of the Rother and the Meon." [2]

" In the situation of some of the Celtic tumuli in this county we find a trace of the reverence of the Celts for water sources, as emblematical of a new and revivyfying

Burials near Springs.

life. The custom of burial near springs, both occasional and permanent, has survived in some instances in this county until our own time. The stream at Holybourne, near Alton, rises in considerable volume from the church-yard itself." [3]

Celtic words.

" The Celts who occupied Hampshire have left behind them some of their language. To this day many of the water names in the County, the names of springs, rivers, ponds and lakes, have been derived from the names which the prehistoric races gave them.

---

[1] Shore's *History of Hampshire*, p. 1, 2.
[2] *Notes and Queries*, vol. vi, p. 122, 3.   [3] *Ibid.*, vol. vi, p. 123

" In this neighbourhood, *Gwy* or *Wy*, water, occurs in the river Wey.

" *Ac* and *Ach*, a spring or watercourse name, occurs in Ashley, and Ashdell.

" *Wysg*, another water name, occurs in Isington, Isnage, and perhaps in Tisted, anciently Isted or Ystede.

" *Curn*, a hollow between hills, occurs amongst others in Stancombe and Kitcombe.

" The Celtic word, *Ock*, occurs in Ockhanger, now Oak-hanger."[1]

" The most enduring remains which the Romans have left in Hampshire are the ruins of cities, villas, and the remains of their great roads. The chief cities are Silchester, Winchester, and Porchester."[2] *Romans.*

Alton certainly was in existence at the time of the Romans, as traces of Roman settlements have been discovered in the town and neighbourhood. At Westbrook House, Messrs. Dyer's yard, the Butts, etc. ; also at Bonhams, Neatham, Freeze End, Alice Holt, Binsted, Kingsley, Selborne, and Blackmoor. Amongst the discoveries may be mentioned a quantity of pottery fragments and encaustic tiles, urns, lachrymatories, or tear bottles, bones, signet rings, bronze, Roman, or Etruscan scarabæus, fibulæ, or brooches for the toga, an old Roman horseshoe, and coins ; also some Roman hollow bricks from Old Alresford. Many of these specimens are to be seen in the Curtis Museum. *Roman remains.*

" About 560 to 600 the Saxons began to form their numerous County tuns or townships. Winchester became their chief tun ; its alternative name of Winton appears to have been given to it by early settlers. Aulton, with others, was probably among the earliest of the primitive West Saxon townships."[3] *560. Townships.*

In 802 Egbert came to the throne, and his reign is an epoch in English History, for he established his authority over the whole county, and made Winchester his capital. *King Egbert 802.*

[1] Shore's *History of Hampshire*, p. 35 and 36.   *Ibid.*, p. 45.   *Ibid.*, p. 50.

It appears that King Egbert left land at Alton to the Monastery of St. Peter and St. Paul, Winchester ; the deed of gift is written in Latin and Anglo-Saxon. I here give the translation, which I have obtained from the British Museum :—

"Translation of the grant by King Egeberct to the Monastery of St. Peter and St. Paul, Winchester, of land at Æweltune, or Alton, co. Hants, 19th August, and 26th December, A.D. 825; with subsequent lease of the land by Bishop Stigand, A.D. 1047 and 1052.[1]

"This is Aweltun's land-charter and the fifteen hides' testimony which King Egbyrht gave to Old-Minster of Winchester for his soul's sake, for the love of God and His glory, and that of His blessed Apostles, St. Peter and St. Paul, for an eternal inheritance.

"The authority of the Old and New Testament declares that the provident dispensation of our Saviour and Lord Jesus Christ has elected all His Saints pre-ordained to eternal life before the making of the world : from among whom He has set before the universal church, which He has redeemed with His blood, two luminaries, that is to say, Peter the blessed prince of the Apostles, and his co-Apostle Paul, unto whom especially he has granted power of binding and loosing both in heaven and on earth, in order that they may receive all the faithful, according to the merits of good works, into eternal tabernacles, but by their word only they may drive away the unfaithful and the adversaries of truth from entering the kingdom of heaven.

"Wherefore I, Egeberct, endowed with royal dignity, desire to be found faithful among the faithful, and desiring to be made a participator with the faithful in the kingdom of the heavens by the intercession of so great Apostles, do grant for ever to Almighty God, a certain portion of land which my predecessors and relatives have left to be possessed by me by hereditary right, to wit, fifteen hides in a place which is customarily called Æweltune by the inhabitants. And I bestow this portion upon the Old-Minster and the Church of the same blessed Apostles Peter and Paul, in the city of Winchester, to the use of the family which devoutly therein, for the health of the whole Christian people, serves Christ.

[1] Cartularium Saxonicum, No. 390.

"'This land, forsooth, a certain most faithful one among my prefects, named Burhghard, formerly held of my gift, but having afterwards died without issue left the same land without disposing of the inheritance, for there was no one surviving him, and thus that land with all its boundaries reverted to me who formerly possessed it, in accordance with judicial decree of my nobles. But I lifted up my eyes and my hands to God the lofty Creator and possessor of heaven and earth, and being mindful of the benefits which He has thought worthy to confer upon me with bounteous hand, I have granted the same land to the aforesaid Old-Minster to be held in right for ever for love of Him, and for the everlasting redemption of my soul and the souls of all my successors. I also confirm this my gift, corroborating it, at the desire and suit of Wigleyn, bishop (of Winchester), with this condition, that no one among secular men presume to trespass upon the aforesaid land nor fraudulently by encroaching take away the little fields adjacent to the same land, but as long as the orbit of this transient age rolls on, let this land itself be under the dominion of the Old-Minster, with the hills and woods, meadows and fields, all other things appertaining thereunto according to the ordinances of old times being added to it. Hereto also I, the aforesaid King, have taken care to increase and multiply this alms for the love of God, and of His Apostles whose tongues have been made the keys of heaven, and therefore I grant to the land aforesaid freedom from all secular charges and also from all earthly services be they small or great, except that which is common to the whole of the people, to wit, expedition and repairs of bridge and castle.

"But if any one shall have wished to increase and amplify this my gift, may God Almighty increase his part in the book of life; on the other hand, if anyone shall have taken it away, let him know that he shall be consumed in the terrible trial, yea, and that he shall render account in the day of judgment before God and His Angels and all the Saints.

"These are the boundaries of the fifteen hides appertaining to Aultune.

"These are the land boundaries to Aweltune. First from the westernmost spring which is called Bradew[e]ll or straight up to the old highway on the west of Woden's barrow. Then to a stone at Cheorlcumbe's head, then to a stone at Woncumb beneath his

topmost hollow, then over randown to the old dike of Æfen
where lieth on the other side a little crundel (cairn), then to the
common gore outside the dike where it again runs into the riad
or red gate, then to a large stone before the link's eastern head,
then to another large stone on the way in the middle of the
valley's bottom which lies out on Wodde's gate, then to a crundel
on the southern part beneathward, then up over the down to a
thorn tree [which] stands in on the dike to the east of Ciceling
way, then along the link from Moxe's down to the old-wall-way to
washing-way beneathwards to the dike, then to wic-lea, then to a
link's head at Beorhtnoth's boundaries, then straight on to the rough
link, then along the link to the lea of the tribe of Heathabriht,
beneathwards, then to an old hollow way along the glade to
Æwelford, then along the brook by the old water bed again to the
spring.   From Moxe's down southwards to the dike, then along
the dike, then to old calf mere, then from the dike to the middle-
most clump of bushes, then to Howere's or the wear's lea upwards,
then along the ride to the little gore midwards, then along the
warp to the highway, then to the dike corner, then along the dike
to Creoda hill, then to the highway against the fifteen acre [field],
then from there along the highway to Tasa mead ; and the heath-
field all common."

Now the beginning of this Charter was written when
King Ecgbergt conducted the army of the Gewissi against
the Britons to the place called Criodan-tree, in the year of
the Lord's Incarnation, 825, in the third indiction, the 14th
of the kalends of September, under attestation of his
bishops and nobles, whose names are read below on the
surface of this sheet.

Afterwards, the text of the privileges of this land was
written at Homtun [Southampton], on the 7th of the
kalends of January, when we celebrate the Nativity of
St. Stephen, the proto-martyr, on the second day of the
Lord's incarnation, under presidency of King Ecgbergt,
together with the bishop Wigthegn and the rest of the
councillors, whose names are noted annexed below.

All these things were translated in the year of the
Lord's Incarnation, 826, in the fourth indiction, in the four-
and-twentieth year of King Ecgbergt, and the fourteenth of
his dukedom.

These are the names of those who were consenting to the testimony of this privilege.

"I, Ecbbert the King, by corroborating this my gift and liberty of the aforesaid land with the sign of the benign cross of our Lord Jesus Christ, confirm it with my own hand, and strengthening it again and again with the little mark of the cross of Christ, confirm it.

Mark of the hand of Bishop Wigthegn.
Mark of the hand of Bishop Alestan.
Mark of the hand of Bishop Hereferth.
Mark of the hand of the Earl Burghard.
Mark of the hand of the Earl Welfhard.
Mark of the hand of the Prefect Monnede.
Mark of the hand of the Prefect Huna.
Mark of the hand of the Prefect Wethelm.
Mark of the hand of the nobles of King Ecbbert [who] have confirmed this.

"Here is shown on this writing the Contract that Bishop Stigand and the Convent of the Old Minster made with Wulfric, when they leased to him the two hides of land and a yard at Aweltune and at Weatha Island (Isle of Wight?), three yards and the mead which belongs to the tributary land, and two vouched leas and [pasture?], for ten cows with the lord's, his sheep leas after the lord's, for his life and one man's life after him, making the best pecuniary arrangements that he can (?).

"This is witnessed by Stigand the bishop and Godwine the Earl, and the convent of the Old Minster and Ælfwine the abbot, and the convent of New Minster and all the shire-thegns of Hampshire. These writings are triplicate, one is at Old Minster, and the second is at Wilton, and the third Wulfric holds."

From the same source I have obtained a translation of the will of a person named Ceolwen, who bequeaths land at Alton to the convent of Winchester.

"Ceolwin makes known by this writing that she gives the land at Alton, the fifteen hides that her lord left to her, and it was acquired by him in lawful ownership in witness of King Ælfred. Now she gives it, after her day, to the convent at Winchester for their refectory at the bishop's see, with so much property as may then be fitting, on condition that they remember the souls of her

[marginal note:] Grant of land by Ceolwin.

and Osmod, as they think just and befitting on his commemoration day, which is seven nights before Rogations. And she enjoins them, in the names of God and St. Peter that the convent never give it from their refectory for any moneys, unless they give it for other land which may be more handy and convenient. And the convent has promised her to settle so that Wulfstan, her brother's son, have a hide of rent-free land the while that he lives."

The Saxon translation of the Latin is equivalent to the above. The boundaries are the same as in the previous charter, with a few unimportant variations.

Translation of the will of Ceolwen, widow of Osmod, bequeathing land at Alton to the convent of Winchester, with condition for anniversary commemoration.

CEOLWENN'S BEQUEST OF AWELTUNE.

"Ceolwen shows in this charter that she grants the land of Aweltune, that is, fifteen hides which her husband leaves to her, and for which (one gave him a price) or a price was given to her, under witness of King Ælfred. These, therefore, she grants to the convent of Winchester after her decease for the refectory of the bishop's see, together with so much money which she shall die possessed of, upon that condition that they be mindful of her and of the soul of Osmod, as they shall think fit, at her or his anniversary, that is, the seventh day before Rogations. She also stipulated in the name of the Lord and of St. Peter, that the same convent may never sell the same land for any money, unless perchance for other land which may be nearer or more useful to them. Moreover, the same convent promised her that they would take care that Wulfstan, her brother's son, should have a certain hide free as long as he shall live."

A. D. 901.
King Alfred.

"Alfred's Will is of special Hampshire interest, for in it we read of his disposal of certain lands in this County nearly a thousand years ago. To his eldest son, afterwards King Edward, he left his land at Hurstbourne, subsequently known as Hurstbourne Tarrant, Sutton, probably that known later on as Bishop's Sutton, and Alton." [1]

"King Alfred made a general collection of laws, and formed them into a book called 'Liber Judicialis, or Dom.

---

[1] Shore's *History of Hampshire*, p. 82.

Boc,' and it was deposited in the Palace of Winchester. Here it remained at the Conquest, and seemed to have given William the idea, and indeed was the ground work of the general survey he afterwards caused to be made. This work was called 'Domesday Book,' and was compiled in 1085–6." [1]

Domesday Book.
A. D. 1085–6.

Alton appears to have been the scene of a battle at the last Danish invasion, and is spoken of in Dean Kitchin's *Winchester*, as follows :—

Danish Invasion about A. D. 980.

" When Olaf of Norway and Swein the Dane, joining hands, ravaged the western districts, Æthelred, incapable of making any stand, decided to offer Olaf tribute and friendship, and the fearless Bishop Ælfeah carried the message of peace to the fierce Norwegian. His mission was successful, and for a time the land had peace. But Swein, the apostate, a fierce foe to Christendom, made no promises, and when Olaf perished in the year 1000, he returned and ravaged Hampshire. A battle was fought at Alton ; thence he passed to Whitchurch, thence to the Worthys, at the very gates of Winchester." [2]

Æthelred.

Alton was also the scene of a sanguinary battle between the Saxons and Danes in 1001. In Samuel Lewis's *Topographical Dictionary* it says :—

A. D. 1001. Battle between Saxons and Danes.

" Alton is noticed in the *Saxon Chronicle* as the scene of a sanguinary battle which was fought between the Saxons and the piratical Danes, who having landed on this part of the coast in 1001, plundered and laid waste the country till they reached this place, at that time called ' Aethelinga-dene,' where the men of Hampshire had assembled in order to oppose their further progress. In this battle, the result of which was favourable to the invaders, sixty-one of the Saxons are said to have been killed, and on the part of the Danes a much greater number were slain, but they, notwithstanding, remained in possession of the field of battle, whence they marched northwards." [3]

Æthelinga-dene.

" In King Edward the Confessor's time Altone was a

1041. Royal Manor in King Edward the Confessor's time.

[1] *Domesday Book for Hampshire.* p. 4.   [2] *Winchester*, Dean Kitchin, p. 37.
[3] Samuel Lewis's *Topographical Dictionary.*

royal manor, and Editha, or Eadgyth, King Edward's queen, was Lady of that Manor." [1]

" In her days it was reckoned at ten hides, but the villains who occupied it paid upon only five, just as afterwards, in 1084, the abbot held in demesne five hides not subject to hidage. Four teams belonged to the manor. In demesne were one team, eleven bordmen, two slaves with two teams, half a mill worth 4s. 7d., two acres of meadow, and wood for fencing. The manor was in 1066 worth £6, and £7 in 1084." [2]

1066. " It appears that half of Alton, with its church, and other five hides of land with a church, were given by King William to Hyde Abbey in exchange for certain other lands. Thus it was that whilst Alton Estbrook, belonged to the Abbey of Hyde, Alton Ansteney was held by the monks of Battle Abbey." [2]

1084. " In 1084, Hyde Abbey held Aultone in Neteham Hundred." [2]

A. D. 1066.
King Harold. " The manors of Hampshire which were held by Harold, before he became king, and the royal demesnes which passed into his possession on the death of King Edward, were no doubt required to furnish men for the English army at Hastings ; and there can be little doubt that men from Odiham, Quarley, and Wallop were there, and also that a more numerous contingent of Hampshire men were there from the royal demesnes of Andover, Basingstoke, Kingsclere, Broughton, Alton, Meonstoke, Hurstbourne, Ealing, Sombourne, Selborne, and many other places." [3]

A. D. 1066. " At the time of William the Conqueror, the land at Binsted, which was part of the great manor of Alton Westbrook, was forest, and was in the hundred of Neatham. It was the home of the wild bull and wild cow, and probably of the wild boar and herds of deer ; and the land of Wolvemere (now Wolmer) shows that wolves were common too." [4]

[1] Gilbert White's *History of Selborne*, p. 307.
[2] Woodward and Wilks' *History of Hampshire*, vol. iii.
[3] Shore's *History of Hampshire*, p. 100.
[4] *Hampshire Notes and Queries*, vol. vi, p. 5.

In one of the new volumes of the Hampshire Record Society, I find a facsimile of the original grant by King William I to Ryuuallonus, Abbot of New Minster, of the Churches of Autune, or Alton, and Clara, or Clere-Regis, co. Hants.[1]

Translation (p. 3) :—

"I, William, by power of the grace of Almighty God, King of the Angles, to all my faithful dwelling in Anglican regions, Will it to be known that I grant to Saint Peter of the New Monastery, and to Ryuuallonus, Abbot of the same Convent, and also to the monks attending upon divine service therein, the Church of Alton, with five hides[2] (of land) and tithes, and with other revenues which belong to the aforesaid Church ; and furthermore the Church of Clere, with four hides and one rod of land, and with tithes and other revenues which belong to the aforesaid Church. Therefore the aforesaid Churches with lands and whatever is contained in them, I grant to Saint Peter and Abbot R. to be free, just as that land of the burying place of the Convent before named was the property of St. Peter and his monks, and free from all service, which I received by exchange from the Abbot for the building of my palace, and for which I make that gift as has been already said. Now if any presumptuous person shall desire to resist the Church of Saint Peter and our grant, and to make that gift of no effect, let him be punished with the penalty of excommunication for ever, with the profane. And that this gift may be held valid and of perpetual obligation I myself make this mark with my own hand."

Grant of land by King William. A. D. 1087.

NOTE.—" At the foot of the Charter is an irregularly formed cross roughly made with a thick pen or split stylus, evidently by one unaccustomed to writing. It appears to be the actual mark made by William the Conqueror, to which allusion is made in the concluding sentence of the deed. The introduction of the text of this Charter between two portions of the Scriptures, upon a blank place in the leaf, seems to have been purposely made in order to mark the solemn ratification of the exchange of possessions entered into between the King and the Abbot, and it is difficult to imagine that this cross would have been placed here as a trick or for any fraudulent purpose."

[1] *New Minster and Hyde Abbey*, by Walter De Gray Birch, F.S.A.

[2] This is probably the property mentioned in Domesday Book, occupied by Herding, etc.

From the same source I have obtained the following grant, of which I give the translation :— [1]

"Grant by Rinuallo, Abbot of New Minster, to the poor and pilgrims of the land, *i.e.*, Manor of Alton, co. Hants, A.D. 1080—1087.

"I, Rinuallo, by the grace of God, Abbot of the Monastery which is called the New Monastery of St. Peter, have granted, with the consent of the brethren, for the relief of the poor and pilgrims, the land which is called Aweltona, in perpetuity, which the King W. gave to us in exchange for the burying ground of our Church, on which his palace has been built.

"*First*, for the soul of the king himself and his wife and children ;

"*Next*, for myself and for all the brethren under my charge ;

"*Lastly*, for all the benefactors of this place.

"Now the witnesses of this donation are Walcelinus (Walkelyn), Bishop, and Hugo, Viscount, and Godefredus, Prior, and Osborne de Ow, and William de Guirices, and Robert Corā, and Teotsel, and Walter Scot, and John, and William, and Benedict, and the rest of the servants of the Abbot.

"Now if anyone at anytime shall have secretly taken away the gift from the support of the poor and pilgrims, let him be subject to excommunication for ever, and be condemned in hell with Dathan and Abiram, and Judas and Nero, and with those who said to the Lord God, Depart from us for we have no knowledge of your ways.—Amen."

A battle seems to have been on the verge of being fought at Alton, in the time of Henry I.

" When Henry I usurped the throne which belonged to Robert, the latter in 1101 landed at Portsmouth, and then marched on Winchester. On arriving there he prepared to besiege it, but hearing that the Queen had just given birth to a son, he proceeded towards London, declaring that, 'Villain would he be who should attack a lady in such a case.' At Alton Henry met him, and another battle would have been fought but for Anselm, who by careful negotiations brought the brothers to terms. A treaty was therefore signed at Alton by which Robert consented to renounce his right to England for a pension of 3000 marks a year." [1]

" John, both before and after he became king, appears to have been very fond of hunting, and considering how much he travelled from place to place, he spent a considerable part of his time in the Hampshire forests. Traditions of his hunting expeditions survive at Southampton, at Freemantle near Kingsclere, at Odiham, and at Worldham near Alton." [2]

A. D. 1199. John.

" Tradition says that King John resided just upon the verge of Woolmer, at Wardlcham, on a regular and remarkable mount, still called King John's Hill and Lodge Hill ; and Edward III had a chapel in his park, or enclosure, at Kingsley." [3]

It is generally supposed in this neighbourhood that King John's hunting box stood where Lode Farm now stands at Kingsley.

" In June, 1204, King John was at Alton, thence going to Winchester and Kingston. From Alton, on June 21st, he sent his order that to his huntsman, Richard Hare (Lepsori), should be paid 10s. to buy himself a gown. We find him there again on March 13, 1217." [4]

1204.

THE HUNDRED OF NETEHAM.

During the eleventh century, Neatham appears to have been a more important place than Alton, for in Domesday Book the Hundred of Neatham is mentioned sixteen times, whilst Alton is only spoken of twice. It also had a market or fair. " This market, with one at Titchfield, and at Basingstoke, are the earliest recorded markets in Hampshire." [5]

Hundred of Neteham.

IN NETEHAM HUNDRED.

" The king holds Neteham in demesne. It was held by King Edward. The number of hides has not been

1041.

---

[1] *Winchester:* Dean Kitchin.   [2] Shore's *History of Hampshire,* p. 120.
[3] Gilbert White's *Selborne,* p. 309.
[4] Woodward and Wilks' *History of Hampshire.*
[5] Shore's *History of Hampshire,* p. 149.

ascertained. Here are 52 ploughlands, 5 ploughlands are in demesne ; and 54 villagers and 26 borderers occupy 47 ploughlands. Here are 16 servants, and 8 mills and a half, which pay 4 pounds 14 shillings, wanting 3 pence, and a market which pays 8 pounds ; and 15 acres of meadow. The woods furnish 150 hogs. It was worth in the time of King Edward and afterwards 76 pounds 16 shillings and 8 pence. It is now valued at the same sum ; but it pays a rent of 118 pounds 12 shillings and 9 pence." [1]

In Neteham Hundred.

1041.   " The Abbot of St. Peter's de Wincester holds Aultone. It was held by Queen Eddid in the time of King Edward. There were then 10 hides, and the villagers, who dwelled there were assessed at 5 hides. The abbot has now 5 hides in demesne, which were not assessed. Here are 4 ploughlands ; 1 ploughland is in demesne, and 11 borderers and 2 servants employ 2 ploughs, and half of a mill, which pays 4 shillings and 7 pence, and two acres of meadow. Here is a copse for fencewood. It was worth in King Edward's time 6 pounds ; it was afterwards, and is now worth 7 pounds." [2]

" Of this manor of Aultone, the king holds 5 hides in his own hands, which are occupied by Herding ; but he is not assessed. The county jury affirm that he came in possession of this unjustly, in exchange of a house with the king ; because the house was the king's own." [3]

" Neteham, Haliborne, Hanstige, Greteham, Ciltelei, and Selesborne, all belong to Neteham Hundred, and were
1034.   held by the king in 1084. Under the Confessor, Lauch held Cittelei, and Ulward Haliborne. The Confessor himself held Neteham, and Queen Eddid the other manors.

" Besides these holdings just mentioned there belonged to Neteham Hundred, the manors of Acangre, Benestede, Ferendone, Froli, Newentone, Nortone, Werildeham, and many others." [4]

[1] *Domesday Book*, p. 5.   [2] *Ibid.*, p. 87.   [3] *Ibid.*, p. 89.
[4] Woodward and Wilks', p. 309.

There was a monastery at Neatham. It was an off- ^{Neatham Monastery. A.D. 1135.}
shoot from, and connected with, Waverley Abbey, which
was founded by William Giffard, Bishop of Winchester,
on Christmas day, in the year 1128. The monks, twelve
in number, came with John their abbot from the Cistercian
convent of D'Aumane, in Normandy.

" King Stephen gave the monks at Waverley, Neatham near Alton, and the church of Farnham, and his gift
was confirmed to them by Henry III in 1239."[1]   " The
monks came there and bought 150 acres more land with
the money which the king's sister gave them, and there
they built a grange and an oratory to say their prayers in,
and had land adjoining the road from Worldham to
Binsted."[2]

" By permission of William de Ralegee, Lord Bishop of ^{A.D. 1250.}
Winchester, and of Peter de Ryeval, Rector of the church
of Alton, it was granted to us this year to celebrate divine
service in the oratory, which is within the bounds of our
grange at Netham, all right and authority belonging to the
Bishop of Winchester, together with an indemnity to the
mother church of Alton, and the chapel of Haliburn being
reserved, *i.e.*, in this manner. That we there celebrate
without beating of bells and distribution of sacraments to
our brethren. That we do not receive the confessions of
secular persons there, except at the point of death, but
that all our domestics and servants at the grange resort to
the chapel of Haliburn for hearing divine service, and for
receiving the sacraments of the church, and that they remain subject to the same as heretofore."[3]

ALTON GOVERNED BY BAILIFFS AND BURGESSES.

" In the reign of Henry III Alton was governed by ^{1216. Henry III.}
bailiffs and burgesses."[4]

" By an order dated from Freemantle, September 19th, ^{1205.}

---

[1] *Waverley Abbey*, by Rev. C. Kerry, pp. 2, 36.
[2] *Hampshire Notes and Queries*, vol. vi, p. 5.
[3] *The Annals of Waverley*, by Rev. C. Kerry, p. 54.
[4] *Woodward and Wilks*, p. 308.

1205, the Sheriff of Hants was desired to let William de Cornhill have at Michaelmas £30 from the farm of Alton, and two marks more at another time. On Nov. 4th, 1205, an order sent from Freemantle advertised the barons of the exchequer that quittance had been given to William for the said monies which he had received from the sheriff.

1207. "A further letter of Oct. 15th, 1207, apprised the sheriff that the king had given Robert de Venuz to farm all his land at Alton, retaining for himself the woods and their profits."

"Many large estates in Hampshire were held under the obligation of making suit at the king's Hundred Courts. Thus the lord of West Worldham manor, etc., had to appear at Alton Hundred Court." [1]

"The lord, or his deputy held his great court twice a year at least, and one in Alton every fortnight, and all the tenants attended and made their complaints." [2]

"Many places in Hampshire had the right of holding a court-leet in addition to the manor court: it could make its own arrangements for the assize of bread and ale, appoint its own ale taster, and usually had also the right of free gallows." "The Abbot of Hyd, who had exercised the privilege of free gallows and assize of bread and ale at Alton, had to prove his claim to same." [3]

"The services on the manors which the tenants had to perform for the lords were numerous.

"East Worldham was held by the sergeantry of bearing a marshal's wand before the king." [3]

"Woolston was held by the service of finding an archer, armed and furnished, to serve the king for forty days in England, and part of the land at Bentley was held by a similar service.

"Alton was also held by the service of three knights, and as often as wars occurred, there must have been the usual preparation for despatching these warriors from that town." [3]

[1] Shore's *History of Hampshire*, p. 165.
[2] *Hampshire Notes and Queries*, vol. vi.
[3] Shore's *History of Hampshire*, pp. 153, 156, 157.

THE DISTRICT OF ALTON, THE RESORT OF ROBBERS.

"The District of Alton is known to have been for a very long period the resort of robbers. There is a spot in the Parish of Bentley, and close to the forest of Alice Holt, to which the word 'pass' would not be inapplicable ; but it is more than probable that the word is used in the sense of road or passage, as ordinarily applied at the present day. The abode of Adam Gurdon, who was disinherited and outlawed with other adherents of Simon, Earl of Leicester, has been described as 'a woody height in a valley near the road between the town of Alton and the castle of Farnham.' This region was not disafforested until the end of Henry's reign, and was a favourite ambush for outlaws, who there awaited the merchants and their trains of sumpter horses travelling to or from Winchester. Even in the fourteenth century the wardens of the great fair of St. Giles, held in that city, paid five mounted sergeants-at-arms to keep the pass of Alton during the continuance of the fair, according to custom."[1]

A. D. 1267. Adam Gurdon.

It is evidently to some such personage that the allusion is made in the quotation :—

"Poverte myght passe withouten peril of robbynge."

The above explanation is made quite certain by William's allusions to Winchester Fair, where Peace is described as being robbed on his way to St. Giles' Down, whereon Winchester Fair was held :—

"Ye, thorugh the pass of Aultone
Poverte myght passe
Withouten peril of robbynge,
For where poverte may paas,
Peace followeth after."[2]

"Against this robber-knight, Prince Edward, desirous of putting an end to the troubles which had so long harassed the kingdom, pursued the arch-rebel into his fastnesses ; attacked his camp ; leaped over the entrenchments, and singling out Gurdon, ran him down, wounded

---

[1] *Account of Domestic Architecture* (thirteenth century), p. 107, by T. Hudson Turner.

[2] Skeats' notes to the *Vision of William concerning Piers Ploughman,* p. 334-5 (a poem written by William Langland).

him, and took him prisoner. He raised the fallen veteran
from the ground, he pardoned him, he admitted him into
his confidence, and introduced him to the queen, then lying
at Guildford, that very evening. This unmerited and un-
expected lenity melted the heart of the rugged Gurdon at
once ; he became in an instant a loyal and useful subject,
trusted and employed in matters of moment by Edward
when king, and confided in till the day of his death."[1]

"Sir Adam seems to have inhabited the house now
called Temple, lying about two miles east of Selborn
church, which had been the property of Thomas Makerel."[2]

A. D. 1272.   "Sir Adam was made Warden, 'Custos,' of the forest
of Wolmer."[3]

"He still appears to have indulged in some depreda-
1282.   tions, as in 1282 we find a 'distringas,' ordering him to
restore to the bishop of Winchester some lands in Hawkley and a mill."[4]

"We are still reminded of the high hand with which de
Gurdon directed matters in this portion of Hampshire, more
than 600 years ago, by a tablet on the cottage, which was
formerly a mill, at Hawkly, which tells us that this is
Hockley mill, ancient mill of the bishops of Winchester,
taken from them by Sir Adam Gurdon, given back under
King Edward, 1280 A.D."[5]

A. D. 1295.
Hampshire
represented in
Parliament.
"Hampshire was first represented in Parliament in 1295,
when four knights of the shire attended at Westminster.
Two burgesses were also sent to this Parliament for the first
time by Winchester, Southampton, Portsmouth, Andover,
Alresford, Overton, Alton, Basingstoke, Yarmouth and
Newport combined as one borough."[6]

"In the early parliaments which met between 1297 and
1306–7, Alresford, Basingstoke, Odiham, Overton and
Alton continued to receive writs."

"Alton was five times summoned to send burgesses to
parliament, but only once obeyed the precept.

[1] *White's* Selborne, p. 336.   [2] *Ibid.*, p. 337.   [3] *Ibid.*, p. 342.   [4] *Ibid.*, p. 344.
[5] Shore's *History of Hampshire,* p. 170.   [6] *Ibid.*, p. 253.

"Geoffrey Tou and Adam de Bradeley sat for the Borough in the twenty-third Parliament of Edward I, held at Westminster. Twice afterwards during that reign and twice during the next to the summons of burgesses from Alton, *Ballivi nullum responsum dederunt.*"[1]

"Edward II granted the privilege of holding a fair at Alton to Edmund of Woodstock, who then held the manor."

A. D. 1307.
Edward II.
Privilege of
holding a fair.

"During the thirteenth and fourteenth centuries the privilege of holding a market or an annual fair in villages and towns was much sought after, and about this time charters were granted by the kings to the lords of the manors of many places in Hampshire to hold fairs, and in some instances both fairs and markets."[2]

TENURE OF LAND.

Amongst the land holders in Alton and neighbourhood may be mentioned "The Priaulx Family, who were connected with Alton as early as 1207."[3]

Land holders,
1207.

"We find in the time of King John, one Gunnora de la Hurn acknowledging that a virgate held by her in Awelton was in the King's Villanage, and that of such land no assize was taken, all which was certified by a jury of Hampshire knights. She further acknowledged that had she a daughter, she could not give her in marriage without redemption, such an acknowledgment being in like cases taken as sufficient evidence of villanage."[4]

"In 1225 we find Margery de Rivers (to whose husband Falk de Breans, son-in-law and heir to Warin Fitz-Gerald, the King, on March 23rd, 1216, had granted Alton) undertaking the payment of her husband's debts to the king, and authorised to collect the debts due to his estate. William Earl of Maundevill (rather W. de Mandeville, Earl of Essex?) was ordered to account to Margery for a debt which his brother had owed Falk de Breans."

1225.

"Notices of the Alton holdings of Peter de Pratellis,

13th Century.

---

[1] Woodward and Wilks' *History of Hampshire.*
[2] Shore's *History of Hampshire,* p. 149.
[3] Woodward and Wilks' *History of Hampshire.*   [4] *Ibid.*

William de Pratellis, Maria de Curtenay, Peter's widow, and Robert de Courtenay, her husband, frequently recur in the records of the thirteenth century."

"The town of Awelton was held by William de Pratellis as three knights' fees."

"Among other land holders, notice may particularly be made of John de Venuz, the Abbey of Hyde, Elias of Rochester, the Marshall, the families of Anstey, Heyes, Popham, Agulon, Paynell, etc."[1]

"Some of the chief families in the neighbourhood at this time were those of de Poutearche at Newton, Gurdon at Selborn and Tisted, Maudit at Hartley Maudit, de Venuz at East Worldham, Paynell at Oakhanger, and de Bardoff at Greatham."[2]

1336—7 A.D.

"An inquisition was held at Alton on the 23rd of January, 1336-7, to enquire about particulars of some land belonging to the late John de Westcote."

"An inquisition on the idiocy of John de Westcote, who ought to have inherited from his father of the same name, land and tenements with appurtenances in Haliburne, Estbrouke, Altone, Westbrouke and other places."[3]

1373 A.D.

"In 1373 a writ was issued for an inquisition as to what damage there might be to the king (Edward III) in William de Trenchant, a Norman alien, holding a certain wood known as Kingeswode, by Aulton or Alton, which Edward I had given him, and other lands in Alton which he had himself acquired."

A.D.

The following is a translation of a grant, dated 11th September, 1496 :—

Henry VII.

"This indenture, made 11th day of September, in the eleventh year of the reign of King Henry VII, between Edward Brocas, son and heir of Sir Thomas Brocas, the Chaplain, on the one part, and William Baynton, of Aulton Westbroke, on the other part, Testifies that the present Edward Brocas hath delivered, etc., to the aforesaid William, all his corner tenement, situated in the market place of Aulton aforesaid called Lady place, with entrance [porta], two gardens, grange and stables

---

[1] Woodward and Wilks' *History of Hampshire.*

[2] Shore's *History of Hampshire*, p. 164.

[3] *Crondal Records*, by the Hampshire Record Society.

adjacent, to hold to the end of a term of 80 years, By paying etc., 24 shillings, etc., etc."

" Witnesses, Henry Quyuke, William Kynswell [EastTisted], Robert Felde, William Felder and others. Given at Aulton aforesaid, the day and year above written."

" It is stated that Edith Brocas, of Beaurspaire, who died 1506, married Ralph Pexall. Their son, Sir Richard Pexall, in August, 1546, exchanged with "The King's Majestie" an estate at Alton, which had belonged to Hide Abbey, for another of about the same value. No reason is assigned. It is described as the manor of Alton Estbrook, in the County of Southampton, with land, tenements, etc., which were "late parcel of the possesshone of the late monastery of Hide." Richard received in exchange, scite, circonite, and precincts of the late priorie of Bradenstocke, in the Co. of Wiltshire." 1506 A.D. 1546.

" Richard Holt, who died in 1457, was the owner of Colmer farm, and had land in many other places. In the Inquisition taken after his death, it appears that he held conjointly with his wife Joan, who survived, "Three messuages, half a carucate of land, eight acres of meadow and six acres of wood, with appurtenances, in Aulton Estbrook, in the County aforesaid, of the abbot of the house and church of St. Peter de Hide, next Winchester, but by what service the jurors know not ; and three messuages, three rods of land and four acres of meadow, with appurtenances in Aulton Westbrook, Whatle and Kyngesle, in the County aforesaid, which are held of the Earl of Worcester ; but by what service the aforesaid jurors wholly know not, and the same jurors say that Cristina and Elizabeth are the daughters and nearest heirs of the same Richard Holt." [1] 1457 A.D.

Translations of other Documents connected with Alton.

Chancery Inquisitions, post mortem. 46 *Hen. III, No.* 27.

" Writ dated at Westminster, 27 June, 46 Hen. III [1262], and directed to William de Wintreshull, commanding him to ascertain the value of the crop of wood in Alton, etc." [2] 1262.

---

[1] Woodward and Wilks' *History of Hants.*   [2] British Museum.

"Henry Wyard, Nicholas Swele, John Turstan, Girard de Colemere, Robert del Oure, William de Hincklegh, William de Holeshet, Nicholas Thurstan, Peter de Benested, Et Pistor, Stephen de Kingeslye, Hugh de Westwod, Nicholas Curcy, Hugh Shulder and John le Hayward, jurors, say the crop of the wood of the Lord the King in the glade (passu) of Awelton in which many depredations and homicides are committed, whereby there is great danger to those passing through, is worth at the present time to sell £20. If that wood were cut down and carried away, the place of that wood if reduced to culture might be let to farm for 31s. 8d. The said place contains altogether 95 acres of land, and that each acre if reduced to culture would be worth per annum 4d."

54 *Hen. III, No.* 33.

1262.

Writ dated at Haveryng, 18 June, 54 Hen. III.[1]

"Richard de Westcote, William de Kaneford, Henry Wyard, Nicholas Sevel, John de Westcote, Henry le Butyler, Andrew Brun, Richard le Fraunkelein, William Kempe, William de la Bure, Robert Gausi and Peter le Brun, jurors, say that it would not be to the damage of the king if he were to confirm to the Abbot and Convent of Hide, Winchester, 5 hides of land with the appurtenances in Aulton and the advowson of the church of Aulton, which they have of the gift of William and by the confirmation of Henry king of England, inasmuch as 4 men and the bailiff of the tenement of the said Abbot came once every year to the torne of the Sheriff to keep the peace of the King and twice every year before the bailiff of the King of the hundred of Aulton, to wit, at Laghedaes when they gave to the King 2s. 8d. of 'tuthing pani.'[2] And that the men of the said Abbott shared with the whole hundred of Aulton in murder if it should happen, but they learn that such exaction is against the tenor of their charters and for default of the bailiffs of the said Abbot who ought to defend their his liberties."

---

[1] British Museum.   [2] Tything-penny.

11 *Edw. I, No.* 60.

" Inquisition taken at Aulton on Tuesday next after the 1272. Conversion of St. Paul, 11 Edw. I before William de Ho, Luke de la Gare by the oath of John de Vensyr, Robert de Chil . . . Philip de Heyford, Walter Huse, Geoffrey Fabri, Nicholas Curcy, William de la More, Henry Wylekyng, Robert de Brerle, William Atterhimere, Nicholas de Thuden, Nicholas atte Flode and Clement de Wydehale, who say that the Mill which is called Johanesmulle is held of the Abbott of Huda in villeinage and the course of water and whatsoever thereto belongs is held of the King in chief, paying therefore yearly 4*s.*, whereof Geoffrey Peterich pays 2*s.*, and William Martin 2*s.* The said William made suit at the court of the Lord the King every 3 weeks by reason of the said course. Sir Adam Gurdun holds the fishing in the said watercourse of the King in chief, paying therefore per ann. 6*d.* The king has always been accustomed to take the said suit and service by the hands of the said tenants, and not by the hands of the said Abbot or his ancestors. A certain small moor belongs to the said course and William Martin holds it of the King in chief by the service aforesaid. After the death of Martin the miller, father of the said William, the Queen was in seisin of a heriot and relief by reason of the tenancy aforesaid."

29 *Edw. I, No.* 79.

" Inquisition taken before Thomas de Wordeston, 1272. Sheriff of Southampton, on Wednesday in the Vigil of the Ascension of our Lord, 29 Edw. I, by the oath of John de Venour, John de Thedden, Nicholas Wyard, John de Aulton, William de Rydelefeld, William Purchas, Philip de Heyford, Henry Wylekin, William le Ken (?), William de Aulton, Askecilli de Wodecotes, and John le Somenour, jurors, who say that it would not be to the prejudice of the King if he granted to Nicholas de la Flode 11 acres of land, 2 a. of meadow, and 6*s.* 1*d.* rent in Aulton, which John le Marischal and Robert de Berele held of the King in chief, to hold to him and his heirs of the said King and his heirs for ever by the same services as the said John and Robert held the same. The said land and meadow are held of the King in chief by the service of 9s. and suit at the court of the King in Aulton every 3 weeks, which the heirs of Robert de Berele paid to the King for 1½ virgates of land together with the said 11 a. of land and 2 a. of meadow by the hands of the farmers of the King of the said court of Aulton. The said rent of 6s. 1d. is held by the service of suit at the said court of the king every 3 weeks. The said land and meadow are worth per ann., clear 6s. 8d. Five virgates of land and 1 wood containing 80 a. remain tô the said John besides the said land, meadow, and rent, and are held of the King by the service of 100s. which he paid yearly into the exchequer of the King. The said 5 virgates of land and the said wood are worth per ann., clear 40s., besides the said rent of 100s. There remains to the heirs of the said Robert de Berele 1½ virgates of land besides the said land, meadow, and rent, which are held of the King in chief by the service of 9s. rent and suit at Court ; they are worth per ann., clear 16s."

Chan. Inq., p. m., 10 Edw. II, No. 61.

1317, South t.　　"Inquisition taken April, 10 Edw[d]. II [1317], by the oath of William de Retherfeld, John atte Hacche, Richard Pikard, William Haynes, Henry Wyard, John Freeman, Peter atte Yerd, Ivonis Sprot, William atte Welle, etc., jurors, who say that William Paynel held 60 acres of arable land of the ancient demesne of the King of Aulton by the service of paying to the farm of the town of Aulton 9s. per ann. at the feasts of Easter and Michaelmas by equal portions, and by the service of making suit at the court of the lord the King of Aulton every three weeks for all service ; each acre is worth per ann. 3d. Also 2 acres of meadow, each acre being worth per ann. 18d."[1]

Chan. Inq., p. m., 19 Edw. II, No. 57.

1326.　　"Inquisition taken at Farndon in co. Southampton before Richard le Wayte, escheator, 9 June, 19 Edw. II

---

[1] British Museum.

[1326], by the oath of John de Candevere, William de Rutherfeld, etc., etc., jurors, who say that Richard de Venuz held the manor of East Worldham in co. Southampton of the King in chief, to wit, 2 parts of the said manor by the service of 113s. 4d., and the 3rd part of the said manor is held of the manor of Aulton which is of the ancient demesne of the Crown ; which said manor of Aulton was at the death of the said Richard de Venuz in the hands of the Lady Isabel Queen of England by the service of 50s. 6d. per ann., to be paid at Michaelmas at the said manor of Aulton."

Chan. Inq., p. m., 35 *Edw. III, p.* 1, *No.* 101.

" Inq : taken at Basingstoke 11 Sept., 35 Edw. III [1361]. The jurors say that Simon de Heyes holds 1 messuage and 1 carucate of land in Aulton of Eustace de Abriggcourt, by the service of 27s. 4d. per ann. The said premises are worth nothing per ann. beyond reprises." 1361.

Add. Charters, 27, 762-4.

" Final agreement made in the court of Elizabeth Julers, Countess of Kent, of Aulton Westbrouk on Thursday in the Vigil of St. James the Apostle, 17 Ric. II, before Henry Popham, steward, Richard Estene, William Knyght, Osebert Bucleswell, Richard Smyth, William atte Douere 'seccator,' between Gilbert Bannebury and Thomas Bochard of Aulton, plaintiffs, and John Bartholomewe, turner, citizen of London, and Lucy his wife, deforciants of 1 messuage, 1 shop, and 1½ acres of land in Aulton, whereupon the said John and Lucy acknowledged the said premises to be the right of the said Gilbert and Thomas and delivered the same to them, to hold for ever." 27,762. 1377.

" For this gift the said Gilbert and Thomas gave 12d. for a fine."

" Final agreement made in the Court of Eliz. Julers, Countess of Kent, held at Aulton Westbrouk on Thursday next before the feast of the Epiphany, 3 Hen. IV, before Henry Popham, steward, John Champflor, [?] Richard Estene, Simon Purchas, William Knyght, and others, 27,763.

between John Mountere and Matilda his wife, plaintiffs, and Thomas Dudelyng and Amicia his wife, defendants, of 1 messuage and 1 garden and 1 acre of pasture in Aulton, whereupon the said Thomas and Amicia acknowledged the said premises to be the right of the said John and Matilda, and released the same to them."

"For this gift the said John and Matilda gave 2s. for a fine."

27,764. "Indenture made 1st July, 1 and 2 Philip and Mary, between Robert Oreswell of Odyam in co. Southampton, gent., of the one part, and Nicholas Vaus of the same town, gent., of the other part, witnesses that for £120 paid to him by the said Nicholas, freely gave to him his 2 messuages in Alton Westbroke, in co. Southampton, one of them called the Swanne, and the other wherein Mellys widow now dwells, adjoining the said Swanne, and 1 close of pasture lying near the same extending to the river on the east and upon the highway on the west, and all the evidences which the said Robert has in his keeping concerning the premises; which evidences the said Robert covenants to deliver to the said Nicholas before the feast of Penticost next coming; to hold to the said Nicholas Vaus and his heirs for ever."

27,816. "Richard, King of England, etc., to the bailiffs of Aulton of Elizabeth Julers, Countess of Kent, greeting. We command you that without delay and according to the custom of the Manor of Aulton you see full right done to William le Shote of Halyborne of 1 messuage and 20 a. of land in Halyborne, of which John Milward and Isabella his wife, Peter King and Isabella his wife, have deforced them. Witness Ourself at Haverford, 2 Sept., 18 Richard II [?]."

27,826. "Henry, by the grace of God King of England and France and Lord of Ireland, to the bailiffs of Elizabeth Julers, Countess of Kent, of Aulton Westbroke, greeting. We command you that without delay and according to the custom of the Manor of Aulton, you see full right done to John Chamflour, Esq., of 5 acres of meadow and 2s. rent, with appurts. in Aulton Westbroke, of which John Bronne de Aulton Westbroke and Alice his wife have deforced him.

Witness Ourself at Westminster, 2 March in the 6th year of Our reign."

"Henry, King of England, etc., to the bailiffs of Henry, 27,834. Bishop of Winchester, Edmund Earl of March, Thomas Earl of Arundel, Richard Earl of Warwick, William le Roos Knight, Henry Fitz Hugh Knight, John Grene, and John Feyreby de Aulton, greeting. We command you to see full right done to Robert Danhurst of 1 messuage, 100 a. of land, 6 a. of meadow, and 4 a. of wood, with appurts. in Aulton, of which John Danhurst and Felicia his wife have deforced him.

Witness the King at Westminster, 2 Nov., I Hen. III [?]."

"Release from Robert, son of Seman of Tuddene, to 1240. Warner den Isenhurste, for the sum of one mark, of all his right in the messuage and two acres of arable land in the village of Aultone, which Adam Algar formerly held of Henry de Isenhurste.

Witn: Rich. de Westcote and John de Westcote, brothers, John son of Richard, Geoffrey the Serjeant ('serviente') of the Abbot of Hyde, John Oter, Henry Wyard, William 'papa' [ᵃₚₚ], Rob. de la Wodecote."[1]

"Grant from Thomas de Monasterio to the Prior and 1250. Cannons of Seleburne, in pure alms, of 12d. of annual rent which Nicholas le Draper of Aweltone and his heirs are bound to pay, as he has been accustomed to pay to the grantor, from seven acres of land held by him in Werlham; of which, two and a half lie in le Suthfelde, and extend above the land of Sir John de Venez at one end, and above Heggemere at the other, one acre lies in one 'garstone,' and two and a half in another 'garstone,' between the land of Tulla ('tulle') and that of Robert de Castel, half an acre lies in Svammere, and half an acre in the field towards Netcham.

[1] Extracts from Charters of Selborne Priory, p. 27.

Witn: Sir John de Venuz, Sir John de la Stane, Sir Thomas Makerel, Nicholas Swele, Roger Wilard, Thomas the Forester then bailiff of Aweltone, Matthew de Monasterio, John de Burhunt."[1]

Seal lost.

1274.   " 13 Jany., 'die S. Hillarii epioc.'; at Duntone.

Copy by H[enry de Helingeye], Archdeacon of Winchester, of a return made by his official to N[icholas] the Bishop of Winchester, in pursuance of a Writ from the King, certifying that upon an enquiry made by the rectors of Farendone and Greetham, the vicars of Froyle, Seleburne, and Ymbesete, and the chaplains of Aultone and Benstede, it was found that the rectory of Worldham was not vacant, but was held by Master John de Brideport, who had been instituted by the Bishop of Winchester on St. James' Day, 1262, on the presentation of the Prior and Convent of Seleburne, the true patrons."

Small fragment of one seal ; another lost.

1430.   " 12 Dec., 9 Hen. VI. Confirmation by Richard Tystede, lord of Westistede, to John the Prior of Selborne, of the grant of a way to the Priory, made by his grandmother Alice, widow of Richard de Tychebourne, under date of 25 July, 1364 (No. 242, which is recited at length) ; paying annually to him a quit rent of one clove.

" Witn : Will. Tystede, John Rutherfelde, John Sylver, John Goolde, Stephen Dyer of Aultone, Will. Astille."

Small red seal of arms, indistinct.

Small oval green seal of the deanery of Alton ; a figure kneeling before St. John the Bapt. (holding the device of the Lamb and Flag), with the legend, " S'decana . . . . . Weltone."

Calendar of Patent Rolls, 1281–1292.

1290, June 6th.   " Grant to Eleanor, the King's mother, for life, in
Westminster.   augmentation of her maintenance, of the following manors and farms, which are extended at 1,000*l.*

The manor of Wych, extended at   ...   89*l.* 5*s*
The manor of Aulton, extended at   ...   80*l.* "[2]

---

[1] Extracts from Charters of Selborne Priory, p. 27.

[2] Calendar of Ancient Deeds.   Record office.

Calendar of Patent Rolls, 1327–1330.

"Grant for life to Hugh de Turpynton of the farm of the town of Aulton, co. Southampton. By privy seal." [1]

1330, May 4. Woodstock.

Calendar of Close Rolls, 1307–1313.

"To the Abbess and Convent of Winchester. Order to receive into their house and to veil Matilda, daughter of John le Mareschal, of Aulton, who wishes to receive the habit of their order, they being bound to admit a maiden (puella) of the King's nomination upon his accession." [1]

1308, March 1. Westminster.

To the treasurer and barons of the exchequer :—

"Order to acquit the abbot of Hide, near Winchester, of 100 marks in which he made fine for license to appropriate to himself and his successors the church of Aulton, the King having ordered him to pay that sum to his envoy, Robert son of Payn, then going to the Pope on the King's business, for his expenses." [1]

1310, July 8. Winchester.

"To the sheriff of Southampton. Order to restore his lands and goods to Peter le Taverner, of Aulton, clerk, taken into the King's hands upon his indictment for the homicide of four foreign merchants before John de Foxle and his fellows, justices to deliver the gaol of Winchester, as he has purged his innocence before Henry, Bishop of Winchester, the diocesan, to whom he was delivered according to the privilege of the clergy."

1312, Dec. 26. Windsor.

Add. Rolls, 27, 665–78.

"Court held there on Thursday next after the feast of the Conversion of St. Paul in the 24th year of King Edward the 3rd from the Conquest." [2]

Aulton, 1350.

"Robert Pyngel against Alice, who was the wife of Robert le Bucke of Aulton, of plea of land. By Roger le Gredere. William de Medestede against Alice, who was the wife of Robert le Bucke, of Aulton, of plea of land. By John Purchaz."

"John de Thudden, senior, against Kathirine, who was

Essoins = excuses.

---

[1] Calendar of Ancient Deeds. Record Office.
[2] Add. Rolls, 27, 665–78. Record Office.

the wife of John de Aulton, of plea of land, whereupon an inquisition. By John atte Strete."

" Nicholas atte Lode, of commission. By Thomas the son, clerk. John Mahn, of commission. By John Holewey."

" John le Kete against Robert le Betere and Isabel, his wife, of a plea of trespass. By Robert le Moncke."

" Henry le Wode, 'wesone,' puts himself in mercy for licence of agreement| ^{to agree} with Thomas de Westcote in plea of trespass. A day is given to Thomas de Westcote, plaintiff, and John le Hurt, defendant, of plea of trespass. On the prayer of the parties until the next court."

" Robert le Betere by John Purchaz, his attorney, and Isabel, his wife, in their proper persons, plaintiffs, put themselves against John Kete, of plea of trespass, and the said John is essioned thereupon, and there is given to him a day by his ession here in three weeks from this day. And the same day is given to the said Robert and Isabel."

" The tithing of Aulton present the drawing of blood between William Clerebalt and William le Bryt, to the injury of the said William Clerebalt, therefore in mercy fined."

" The tithing of Aulton present a hue raised between John Ledesye and William de Malmesbury to the injury of the said John, therefore in mercy."

" Alice, who was the wife of Robert le Bucke of Aulton, plaintiff, puts herself by John atte Strete her attorney, against Robert Pynget and Joan his wife, of plea that they render to her 2 acres of land with appurts. in Aulton ; and against William de Medestede, of plea that he shall render to her 2 acres of land with appurts. in Aulton ; and the said Robert and William are essioned thereupon and a day is given them by their ession here in three weeks from this day. And the said Joan came and the same day is given to her, and the same day is given to the said Alice, the plaintiff, etc."

" John le Buche of Aulton, plaintiff, puts himself by his ession against William de Medestede, of plea of land, and the said William is essioned thereupon, and a day is given to him here in three weeks from this day, and the same day is given to the said John by his ession, etc."

" A day is given to Richard le Brut, plaintiff, by the pledge of John le Ropere and John Wyborne, defendant, of plea of covenant. On the prayer of the parties till the next court."

" A day is given to Richard le Brut, plaintiff, as above, and to the said John of plea of trespass. On the prayer of the parties [adjourned] till the next court."

Sum—16*d.*

" 13 November (6 Henry VII) view of Frankpledge.[1]   1490.

"'Amercements.' William Bocher, of Alton, 3*s.* 4*d.* for selling the flesh of bulls that had not been baited.

William Bocher, of Alton, and Richard Bocher, of Alton each, 12*d.*, because they sold bad meat, putrid and old."

2 *Hen. VIII.*

" October. Laurence Eglisfeld, carriage of jackets from   1510. Alton to Waverley, thence to Guildford and Oking, 3*s.* 8*d.*[2]"

13 *Hen. VIII.*

Grants in March, 1522 :—

" 26. Sir Wm. Sandys, Knight of the Body, to be   1522. lieutenant or keeper of Alisholte and Woolmer Forests, Hants, which office was granted by patent, 18 April, 1 Hen. VIII, to Thomas, Earl of Arundell, and Wm. Arundell, lord Matravers, but has been taken into the king's hands by Sir Th. Lovell, justice of the king's forest this side of Trent, in his last eyre in the said county ; to receive annually 15 quarters of oats from his tenants of Alton Estbroke and Alton Westbroke, and five quarters of wheat from the Abbot of Hyde, and to hold a wood court in the said forests, every sixth week, for levying fines, deciding suits concerning the slaying of beasts, etc. Also

---

[1] *History of Basingstoke. Selections from Court Rolls.*
[2] King's Book of Payments. Record Office.

reversion of the manor of Wardelham, Hants, now held by the said Earl and Lord." [1]

Del. Hampton Court, 26 March, 13 Hen. VIII.

S. B.   Pat. p. 1, m. 26.

17 *Hen. VIII.*

1525.
Grants in September, 1525 :—

" 12.   Wm. lord Sandes.   To be keeper of the forests of Alisholte and Woolmer, Hants, with fees, as enjoyed by Tho., late Earle of Arundel, with oats from the tenants of Alton Estbroke and Alton Westbroke. . . . . . ." [1]

Del. Westm., 12 Sept., 17 Hen. VIII. S.B., Pat. p. 2, m. 8.

18 *Hen. VIII.*

1526.
" 24 August, 1526.   Sandys to Wolsey.   Received Wolsey's letter on Sunday, 19 Aug.   Dr. Knight, who was to have presented the ambassadors and Wolsey's letters to the king, fell sick at Alton, and only got to Winchester on Monday morning, so that Sandys presented the packet in place of him. . . ." [1]

18 *Hen. VIII.*

1526.
Grants in May, 1526 :—

" 14.   Lawrence Redman, of Alton Westbroke, Hants mercer.   Protection ; going in the retinue of Lord Berners, Greenwich, 14 May, 18 Hen. VIII, P.S." [1]

20 *Hen. VIII.*

1528.
Grants in December, 1528 :—

" 15.   John Byrcom, alias Bircoon, of Lyse Sturnay, alias of Alton, Hants, butcher.   Pardon for having received from John Yong, of Lysturmy, husbandman, certain cattle stolen by the said John." [1]

Bridewell, 10 Dec., 20 Hen. VIII.   Del. Westm., 15 Dec., P.S., Pat. p. 2, m. 24.

24 *Hen. VIII.*

1532.
" William Button to Cromwell.   The Warden of the New College has granted to the farm of Alton a new lease, which is not delivered until he comes to his audit. . . . ." [1]
Hol., p. 1.

[1] King's Book of Payments.   Record Office.

27 *Hen. VIII.*

"5 July, 1535. Henry VIII . . . . Thursday, 1535.
23 Sept. Alsford to Alton, to dinner, that night to Farnham, and then till Sunday, 14 m. . . . ."[1]

Domestic—Elizabeth, vol. cxxxvii.

"April, 1580. 60–65. Certificates of general musters 1580.
of able men and armour in the divisions of Alton, Pork-
down, Andover, Fawley, Redbridge, and Basingstoke, in
the county of Southampton, Six returns."[1]

State Papers.

"Articles given by Sir Richard Norton, against William 1581.
Pitts, late of Alton, and Benjamin Tychbourne, for sedi-
tious speeches concerning religion and government. Benjamin Tychbourne had countenanced him. Pitts escaped
from Bath gaol."[2]

"A conspiracy to fire beacons; to redress present 1586.
dearth of corn and to rob gentlemen's houses, particularly
Sir. R. Norton's, and to liberate recusants."[2]

"May 15. Justices of part of Hampshire to the 1622. Vol. 130.
Council:— James I.
The smallness of contributions is through the poverty
of the people, not through negligence. Alton division
sends £254. 10s. 4d."[2]

"July 25. Order given for troop under Sir Benjamin 1625.
Tichborn to assemble at Kings lyngate on August 4 and
5. Those under Sir John Compton at Olddown, near
Alton, on the 8 and 9; and Sir R. Norton's troop at Old
Winchester on the 28th."[2]

"The Alton Regiment:— 1637.

Sir Richard Norton's.			Sir John Compton's.		
Officers...	...	6	Officers...	...	6
Halberts	...	10	Halberts	...	10
Corslets	...	47	Corslets	...	36
Muskets	...	50	Muskets	...	50

---

[1] King's Book of Payments. Record Office.
[2] State Papers—Domestic. Record Office.

1640. Domestic.
Charles I
(No. 47, p. 152),
Vol. 453, State
Papers.

" May 12.   Sir Rich. Tichborne, Sir. Rich. Norton, Dep. Lieutenants of Hants, and Jas., Duke of Lennox, and Jerome, Earl of Portland, lords lieutenants of Hants.   We have endeavoured to the utmost to put in execution those directions lately sent us.   We have, with the consent of the Justices of the Peace, sent out warrants for raising cost and conduct money.   In many places we find a readiness to contribute, while others are altogether averse, especially the hundreds of Odiham and Alton, which for the most part refuse to pay anything, as appears by the constable's returns, alleging for their reason that many of their hundreds have heretofore refused to pay the ship money, nothing has been done to them by way of example, and they hope they may as well escape for this. If a speedy course be not taken herein, we suppose that for want of pay the soldiers will be hardly kept from mutining, and ourselves shall receive much prejudice, not only in the money we have already disbursed for the impress, but likewise in our own particular credits, having engaged ourselves for the costs, but most especially it will be a great blemish and disadvantage to the King's service. We therefore desire you to direct some course for redress of this, for preventing the like hereafter." [1]

1640. Domestic.
Charles I
No. 48, p. 118-9.

"Alton, Sept. 30. The Depy. Lieutenants of Hants to the Council.   We rec^d. two letters from you on the 27 inst.; to the one we answer that as yet we have made no excuse for the marching of our troops, nor shall we do so but on just occasion, though we know we have of late had as many charges laid on us as any county in England. And as we have been ever ready to serve his majesty and observe your commands to the best of our ability, so shall we be willing as far as any of his Majesties most loyal subjects, to continue the same, being confident of receiving no heavier charge than we can bear. To the other, we have written to the colonels and captains of the trained bands to be ready to march on a day's warning, and all other things to be prepared fit for such an occasion, also to have the bea-

[1] State Papers.—Domestic.   Record Office.

cons prepared and diligently watched, and if any difficulty arise we will acquaint you therewith. But touching a magazine of powder, we have heretofore written to you that our county never had any except what Queen Eliz[th]. provided, and that was the order delivered to my Lord of Worcester on promise to have it mended, it having grown old with long keeping, but we could never receive any again. We have often written for powder, which the county would willingly take at reasonable rates to exercise themselves in the use of their pieces, and to have some store by them for the defence of the county, etc." [1]

" 14 April. Sir Ed. Nicholas and the Earl of Forth, Lord-General of the King's forces. This bearer, Edmund Parker, late a lieutenant in Sir Jacob Astley's regt., was taken prisoner at Alton, and hath procured liberty to solicit for his exchange for one John Johnson, now prisoner in the Castle here, to obtain which he comes recommended from Sir Jacob Astley. Though his Majesty is not willing to grant this till Sir. Ed. Stradling and Al. Lansford be released, yet when those two gentlemen shall be exchanged it is his Majesties pleasure the said Johnson be released for Lieut. Parker and no other person." [1]
(margin: 1644. Charles I, Vol. 501, No. 51, p. 117.)

" In the times of Queen Elizabeth and King James it was no easy matter for a man to change his residence.
(margin: 1560—1625. Change of Residence in Queen Elizabeth and King James' time.)

" The inhabitants of towns were very jealous of admitting strangers to share their privileges. And so in Farnham, as in other towns, before a stranger was allowed to take up his residence therein, he was obliged to get some citizen of good character to be bail for him. Two such deeds are still preserved amongst the town records."

" In the first John Hockley, yeoman, and Henry Tilly, glover, stand security for 40*l.* for Richard Mayne, butcher, of Alton, who had come to Farnham."

" In the next John Hinton, Thomas Beldam and Alexander Beldam stand surety for John Hunt." [2]

---

[1] State Papers—Domestic. Record Office.
[2] *Farnham*, by Rev. R. N. Milford, p. 44.

ROYALTY AT ALTON.

1101.   "Henry I signed a treaty at Alton with his brother Robert in 1101."

1204. 1217. "King John passed through the town to Winchester in 1204, and visited it again in 1217."

1509.   "In his youth Henry VIII was fond of hunting, and a place in Woolmer Forest now called Lode Farm was a favourite hunting box of this prince. From the frequent visits he paid to it, we are told he got the name of Harry at Lode."[1]

1635.   It appears from the old Churchwardens' and Vestry Books that "Kinge (Charles I) came through yᵉ Towne in April, 1635."

1669.   "King (Charles II) also passed through in 1669."

1684.   "His Maᵗⁱᵉ. James II rode through to Winton and returned in 1684."

CANTERBURY PILGRIMS.

Canterbury Pilgrims.   "The pilgrims of old, bound for the shrine of St. Thomas at Canterbury, some, especially those who came from Normandy and Britany, landed at Southampton, and travelled through the southern counties of Hampshire, Surrey, and Kent. Many of these doubtless stopped at Winchester, attracted by the fame of St. Swithin, the great healing Bishop; and here they would be joined by the pilgrims from the west of England on their way to the shrine of Canterbury. This was the route taken by Henry II, when, landing at Southampton on his return from France, he made his first memorable pilgrimage to the tomb of the murdered archbishop, in the month of July, 1174. And this route was trodden by thousands of pilgrims during the next three centuries, and may still be clearly defined through the greater part of its course, and in Surrey and Kent bears the historic name of the 'Pilgrim's Way.' Few traces of the Pilgrim's Way are now to be found in Hampshire. The route they took on leaving Winchester is uncertain; it is not till we reach Farnham

1174.

---

[1] Shore's *History of Hampshire*, p. 255.

that we find the line of hills along which the Pilgrim's Way runs, but in all probability they followed the Roman road, which still leads to Silchester and London, along the valley of the river Itchen. They in all probability passed through Alresford, and tradition says that the Pilgrim's Way lay through the parish of Ropley, a neighbouring village where Roman remains have been discovered ; and a little further on the same road, close to Rotherfield Park, is an old farm house which still bears the name of ' Pilgrims Palace.' thence through Chawton, Alton, and Farnham." [1]

"Pilgrim's Palace," or place, here mentioned, is now identical with Pelham, the residence of the Misses Lempriere. The name Pelham is derived from the French word *Pèlerin*, signifying Pilgrim. There are also one or two fields close by, known by the name of Pilgrim fields.

LAND BOUGHT IN THE TOWN AND NEIGHBOURHOOD BY WINCHESTER COLLEGE.

"John Baker was a great buyer of lands, investing in that way surplus funds of Winchester College. In 1471 he bought lands in Hawkley, Newton Valence, and Inbershete (Empshot) for £40. In 1480, among others, he bought Holtham and Herdes, in the parish of East Tisted, and Goleigh in Priors Dean. In 1482 he acquired a farm at East Worldham, the manors of Will Hall and Wyards, close to Alton, and lands lying dispersedly in the common fields adjoining that town, a messuage called Stonehouse, in the High Street, and a tenement in Turk Street," [2]

1431.
1471.
1480.
1482.

" Stonehouse " is the house now occupied by Mr. Turner-Smith and part of the next house of Mr. Dykes, property of Winchester College, renewable leasehold.

---

[1] *The Pilgrim's Way from Winchester to Canterbury,* by Mrs. Henry Ady (Julia Cartwright), the Hampshire Antiquarian and Naturalist, vol. 2, p. 19, 20.

[2] Kirby's *Annals of Winchester College,* p. 210.

THE CIVIL WAR.[1]

1642.

During the Civil War that broke out between King Charles I and the Parliament in the year 1642, Alton became involved in several encounters, but one is invested with special historical importance. During the war, the siege of Farnham Castle and Basing House being protracted, and Alton lying somewhat between the two, the Royalist and Parliamentarian troops frequently came into collision. I am indebted to the Rev. G. N. Godwin's *Civil War in Hampshire*, published in 1882, for the following interesting facts :—

"Hearing that Sir William Waller was anxious to march towards the west, Prince Rupert, on February 22nd, 1643, rode out of Oxford at the head of a considerable force, and tried to intercept four guns and seven cartloads of ammunition, which were on their way to join the Parliamentary army. Rupert and his troopers reached Basingstoke and exchanged greetings with the stout old Marquis of Winchester, but failed to secure their prize, Waller having received intelligence of their arrival, and sent orders to the convoy to halt upon its march whilst he himself retreated to Guildford. Detachments of his forces had already reached Winchester and Alton, and orders were at once despatched to recall them. The party from Winchester retired without molestation, but the Alton detachment was not so fortunate. It was 200 strong, and was reconnoitring the roads into Gloucestershire and Wiltshire, and reached Alton on February 22nd. Scarcely had the wearied troopers unsaddled, before 1500 of Rupert's wild riders beset the town. Thinking that resistance would be useless, they cried for quarter, which was scornfully refused ; whereupon they prepared to sell their lives dearly. Having a field piece with them, they loaded it with musket bullets and calmly awaited attack. The cavaliers came boldly within range ; the gun was fired, and when the smoke cleared away, 80 of the assailants were seen to be either killed or wounded, and the rest retreating in con-

[1] *Civil War in Hampshire,* by the Rev. G. N. Godwin.

fusion. Night was falling fast, but on came the attacking party once more. Again did that murderous field piece scatter its deadly hail, and again did 40 soldiers of the king fall *hors de combat.* Darkness put an end to the strife, and the cavaliers deferred their intended capture until the following morning, only to find at dawn that the gallant defenders of Alton had skilfully escaped and fallen back in good order on the main body during the night."

" On Wednesday, September 13th, 1643, an ordinance of Parliament was passed, ordering Sir William Waller to collect forces for the protection of Hampshire. Farnham was the Parliamentarian base of operations, and from thence Sir William Waller determined to advance against Basing. It was resolved to occupy Odiham and Alton, and from thence to proceed by gradual approaches towards Basing, taking possession of or destroying anything that might prove of service to the enemy."

" On November 2nd, Waller was said to have at Farnham and Guildford between five and six thousand men, and had surprised at Alton 100 cavaliers under the command of Colonel Bennett. On Friday, November 3rd, the regiments marched from Farnham towards Alton, and were reviewed by their general on Bentley Green. The " field state " showed that there were present 16 troops of horse, 8 companies of dragoons, 36 companies of foot, and a train of artillery, consisting of ten heavy guns, and six cases of small " drakes." After an hour's halt the march towards Alton was resumed, and that night Elias Archer's regiment was quartered at the little villages of East and West Worldham, two miles distant from Alton. Sir Ralph Hopton's forces retired from Winchester towards Andover and Salisbury at the approach of Waller's army. Saturday, the 4th of November, was a day of rain and snow, which compelled Waller's troops, who had mustered in force about two miles from Alton on the road to Winchester, to return to their quarters. The 5th of November witnessed a great muster in the neighbourhood of Alton, and the army took the road to Winchester, but towards evening,

when about nine miles distant from that city, turned to the
right, halting for the night at the village of Chilton Can-
dover, between Alresford and Basingstoke."

"On Friday, Dec. 1st, 1643, Lord Crawford occupied
Alton with a regiment of horse and another of foot and
began to fortify the town with all the speed he could, and
Sir Ralph Hopton quartered many of his men at Alresford
and Petersfield, which was done in policy to keep them
from Winchester." "The infantry regiment here referred
to, Clarendon says was about 500 strong, but the epitaph
of its Colonel states that it was not less than 1300. It was
under the command of Colonel John Bolle, second son of
Sir John Bolle, who died in 1606. He was an ancestor of
the present Warden of Winchester College, to whom I am
indebted for much information concerning him. This
gallant soldier was a brother of Sir Charles Bolle, of Louth
Hall, in Lincolnshire, who on one occasion concealed himself beneath the arch of a bridge near the gaol at Lowth,
whilst the enemy's troopers galloped unsuspectingly above
his head. He raised a regiment amongst his tenants for the
king, and gave the command of it to his brother John."

"Colonel John Bolle did great deeds at Edgehill and
other places at the head of his regiment, whose ranks, sadly
thinned by the ravages of war and disease, seem to have
been afterwards filled with Welsh and Irish recruits."

"On the evening of Saturday, December 9th, most of
Waller's men were drawn up in Farnham Park, and a party
was that night sent towards Alton, which beat up Lord
Crawford's quarters, and afterwards fell back upon Farnham. But more stirring work was at hand."

"An attack in force upon Alton having been decided
upon, Lieut Archer says :—'Tuesday, December 12th, most
of our men went presently into the town (Farnham) to
refresh and prepare themselves for the service, where,
although they before gave their general consent, many of
them stayed behind, and went not with their colours ;
nevertheless we advanced without them.' "

"During the morning hours of this memorable 12th of December, Lord Crawford had sent a messenger to Farnham asking Sir William Waller to send him to Alton a runlet of sack, promising to send a fat ox in exchange. 'Our worthy Sir William sent in a loving compliment to the Lord Crawford half a hogshead of sack, who mistrusting the matter and the messenger, caused the messenger and divers others to taste thereof, and then caused it to be carefully laid by for his own drinking.' Sir William Waller demanded the promised ox, whereupon Lord Crawford replied that he would bring it himself. Waller fails not at nightfall to go in search of his ox, and instead of a beast, brought away 565 prisoners."

"His men, 5000 in number, mustered without beat of drum in the park at Farnham, and commenced their march about seven o'clock in the evening, going in the direction of Basing House. But after advancing about two miles, the cavalry halted for an hour upon a heath between Crondall and Farnham, and awaited the arrival of the infantry, and thus reinforced continued their march, which was favoured by the hard frost, which at this time lasted for six weeks without intermission. Lieut. Elias Archer says :—' But having marched that way about two miles we returned to the left.' Another eye-witness says that the whole force marched as if towards Basing until one o'clock in the morning, and then faced south towards Alton, between the hills."

"Lieut. Archer says that they 'in a remote way between the wood and hills marched beyond Alton, and about nine o'clock on Wednesday morning, December 13th, came upon the west side of the town, where we had both the wind and hill to friend.' Sir William Waller's scouts were vigilant, so that his main force arrived without attracting observation. *Mercurius Aulicus* (a series of Civil War tracts on behalf of the king, which then served for newspapers) admits that the cavalier scouts had concentrated their attention on the main road leading from Farnham to Alton, not expecting an attack from any other quarter.

Some of Sir William's scouts were captured, but others brought information that Lord Crawford was quartered in the town with between 300 and 500 horse, in addition to the infantry regiment of Colonel John Bolle. Scarcely had they made their report before Lord Crawford and his troopers were both seen and heard galloping at speed out of the town towards Winchester, having promised their comrades of the infantry that they would speedily return with reinforcements. They quitted Alton on the eastern side, but being unexpectedly headed back by the Parliamentariam horse, they galloped back through the town, and rode to the southward direct for Winchester ; whilst in their rear, now sabreing one, now capturing another, rode the pursuing mail-clad squadrons of Sir Arthur Haslerig, known as ' Lobsters ' from their iron shells, and says the stern Puritan chronicler, 'our Foot made the woods ring with a shout.' Three or four cavaliers were slain in the pursuit, which was followed for about half-a-mile through narrow lanes, and about 30 horses and some prisoners were taken by Sir Arthur's men, who then returned and blocked up all the entrances to the town, leaving Lord Crawford and his men to make the best of their way to Winchester."

" Nor were the infantry idle meanwhile. Lieut. Archer says, ' Then Sir William's own regiment of foot, Sir Arthur Haslerig's five companies, and five companies of Kentishmen went on upon the north and north-west side, and gave the first onset by lining of hedges and the like, but could not as yet come to any perfect execution, in respect that our London regiments were not come in sight of the enemy, and therefore they bent all their force against those three regiments and lined divers houses with musqueteers, especially one great brick house near the church was full, out of which windows they fired very fast, and might have done great prejudice to those men, but that when our train of artillery came towards the foot of the hill, they made certain shot, which took place upon that house, and forced them to forsake it. In the meantime our London regiments and four companies that belong to Farnham Castle came

down the hill ; then the Red Regiment and the Greencoats
and the four companies of Farnham Castle set upon a half
moon and a breastwork which the enemy had managed,
and from which they fired very hot and desperately till the
Green Auxiliaries marched on the other side of a little river
into the town with their colours flying, and being in the
wind of the enemy, fired a little thatched house, and so
blinded them that this regiment marched forwards, and
coming in part behind the works, fired upon them, so that
they were forced to forsake the said half-moon and breastwork, which they had no sooner left but presently the
Greencoats and part of the musqueteers of the Red and our
Yellow Regiments entered, while the rest of our regiment
marched into the town with their colours flying.'"

"Another eye-witness, already referred to, says that the
infantry advanced as far as the market place."

"Lieut. Archer continues : ' Now was the enemy con-
strained to betake himself and all his forces to the church,
churchyard, and one great work on the north side of the
church, all which they kept near upon two hours very
stoutly, and having made scaffolds in the church to
fire out of the windows, fired very thick from every place.'"

" The other account says that the Cavaliers, being all
musketeers, retired to the works near the church, ' where
they had double trenches and a half-moon.' The church
and a barn close by were ' chiefest refuge '; and there was
"a very hot fight near two hours by reason of a malignant,
who willingly fired his own barn and other houses.' The
smoke caused much annoyance to the assailants, who lost
about three men ' by reason of which smoke.'"

" The battle word of the Cavaliers was ' Charles '; that
of their opponents being ' Truth and Victory.'"

"' The fight continued,' says Lieut. Archer, ' till divers
soldiers of our regiment and the Red Regiment fired very
thick upon the south-east of the churchyard, and so forced
them to forsake that part of the wall, leaving their muskets
standing upright, the muzzles whereof appeared above the

wall as if some of the men had still lyn there in ambush, and our men seeing nobody appear to use those muskets, concluded that the men were gone, and consulted among themselves to enter two or three files of musqueteers, promising Richard Guy, one of my captain-sergeants, who was the first that entered the churchyard, to follow him if he would lead them. Whereupon he advanced, and coming within the churchyard door, and seeing most of the Cavaliers firing at our men from the south and west part of the churchyard, looked behind him for the men which promised to follow him, and there was only one musqueteer with him. Nevertheless, he, flourishing his sword, told them if they would come the churchyard was their own; then Symon Hutchinson, one of Lieut.-Col. Willoughbie's sergeants, forced the musqueteers and brought them up himself. Immediately on this, one of the sergeants of the Red Regiment, whose name I know not, and therefore cannot nominate him as his worth deserves, brought in another division of musqueteers, who, together with those which were there before, caused the enemy's forces to betake themselves towards the church for safeguard, but our men followed them so close with their halberts, swords, and musket stocks, that they drove them beyond the church door, and slew about ten or twelve of them, and forced the rest to a very distracted retreat. Which, when the others saw who were in the great work on the north side of the churchyard, they left the work and came, thinking to help their fellows, and coming in a disorderly manner to the south-west corner of the church, with their pikes in the rear (who furiously charged on in as disorderly a manner as the rest led them), their front was forced back upon their own pikes, which hurt and wounded many of the men and brake the pikes in pieces. By this time the churchyard was full of our men, laying about them stoutly with halberts, swords, and musket stocks, while some threw hand grenades in at the church windows, others attempting to enter the church, being led on by Sergt.-Major Shambrooke, a man whose worth and valour envy cannot stain, who in the entrance

received a shot in the thigh, whereof he is very ill.' Major
Shambrooke is elsewhere said to have been wounded in the
thigh in the church by the pistol of a prisoner, to whom he
had given quarter. 'Great hopes there is of his speedy
recovery.' An entry having been forced into the church,
the exterior and interior of which still bear many a bullet
mark, Colonel Bolle declared with an oath that he would
'run his sword through the heart of him which first called
for quarter.' Clarendon says that he hoped to defend the
church "for so many hours that relief might be sent to him,
but he had not time to barricade the doors ; so that the
enemy entered almost as soon, and after a short resistance,
in which many were killed, the soldiers, overpowered, threw
down their arms and asked for quarter, which was likewise
offered to the Colonel, who refused it, and valiantly de-
fended himself, till with the death of two or three of the
assailants, he was killed in the place, his enemies giving him
a testimony of great courage and resolution.' According
to a family tradition, the Colonel was shot in the pulpit, but
according to *Mercurius Aulicus* he was knocked on the
head with the butt end of a musket. The *Weekly Account*
of December 20th, 1643, says, ' I am certainly informed
there were not above fifteen pieces found in the pocket of
Colonel Bolles, who, until he fell himself, did bravely en-
courage and lead on his soldiers.' "

"This gallant soldier's epitaph is inscribed on two brasses,
one of which is affixed to a pillar near Bishop Morley's
monument in Winchester Cathedral, and the other is in
Alton Church. It states that the strength of his regiment
was 1300, and that he took refuge in Alton Church with
about 80 of his men ; that the fight lasted six or seven
hours, and that Colonel Bolles killed six or seven of his
assailants before he was slain, together with sixty of his
men. The author of this epitaph, who claimed kinship to
the gallant Colonel, erroneously stated the date of Alton
fight as 1641, instead of 1643, and it has been justly
remarked, ' As no hero was ever perhaps more deserving of
an honourable commendation to posterity; so never perhaps

was there epitaph more devoid of grammar and orthography, than that which is here erected to his memory.'"
It thus concludes :—

"His Gratious Soveraigne, hearing of his death, gave him his high commendation in ye pationate expression, Bring me a moorning scarffe, I have lost one of the best Commanders in this Kingdome,"

> "Alton will tell you of that famous Fight
> Which yᵉ man made, and bade this world good-night.
> His Vertious Life fear'd not Mortality,
> His body must, his Vertues cannot die,
> Because his Bloud was there so nobly spent,
> This is his Tombe ; that Church his Monument.
> Ricardus Boles, Wiltoniensis in Art. Mag.
> Composuit Posuitque Dolens. An. Domi 1689."

According to Lieutenant Archer, "He being slain, they generally yielded and desired quarter, except some desperate villains which refused quarter, who were slain in the church, and some others of them wounded, who afterwards were granted quarter upon their request."

"The Lieutenant says that Waller's loss was 'not above eight or nine at the most, besides what were wounded, and I conceive their loss of men to be about fifty or sixty, most of which were slain in the church and churchyard after we had entered.' *Mercurius Aulicus* says 'that 27 of the king's men fell at Alton, and that only 300 were made prisoners, whilst Waller had 200 men killed in the church and churchyard.'"

"Master Elias Archer says that when all resistance was at an end, the prisoners who had been taken in and about the church were placed in a large barn, which joined to the churchyard, and after the church was cleared of our men, they were all put into the church, and the rest which were taken in several houses in the town were put to them and there they were coupled together and brought to Farnham, the number of them being about 875, amongst whom were about fifty commanders besides horsemen, which were taken in pursuit of the Lord Crawford, who ran away from the town as soon as we gave the first assault upon their works."

Plate III.

ST. LAWRENCE CHURCH, ALTON.— 1830.

" Waller at once employed the inhabitants of Alton to ' slight' or demolish the fortifications which had been constructed in and about the town by the cavaliers."

" Lord Crawford left his hat and cloak behind him at Alton, and owed his escape to the speed of his horse. It will be remembered that he had on the previous day received with due tasting precautions a present of some wine from Sir William Waller. This he also left behind him in his flight, and it was ever afterwards remembered against him that he ' left his sack at Alton.' "

" The following characteristic letters from Hopton and Crawford were read in the House of Commons on Monday, December 18th, together with a letter from Sir William Waller, whose first messenger announcing his victory, had reached London on December 13th." :—

" To Sir W. Waller.—Sir, I hope your gaining of Alton cost you dear. It was your lot to drinke of your own sack, which I never intended to have left for you. I pray you favour me so much as to send me my own chirurgion, and upon my honour I will send you a person suitable to his exchange.

Sir, your servant,   CRAWFORD."

" To Sir W. Waller.—Sir, This is the first evident ill success I have had. I must acknowledge that I have lost many brave and gallant men. I desire you, if Colonel Bolles be alive, to propound a fit exchange; if dead, that you will sende me his corps. I pray you sende me a list of such prisoners as you have, that such choice men as they are may not continue long unredeemed. God give a sudden stop to this issue of English Blood, which is the desire, Sir, of your faithful friend to serve you.

" Winton, 16th December.   RALF HOPTON."

" Clarendon adds :—' The Lord Hopton sustained the loss of that regiment with extraordinary trouble of mind, and as a wound that would bleed inward ; and therefore was the more inflamed with desire of a battle with Waller to make even all accounts. A little more patience, my Lord Hopton, and your wish shall be fully gratified.' "

" It was noticed that Alton was taken at the very time when the Cavaliers at Oxford were making ' bon fyers ' with much triumph for the death of Pym."

E

"On Friday, December 15th, Sir Arthur Haslerig and Sir Gilbert Gerard were ordered by the House of Commons 'to prepare a letter to be written to Sir William Waller, to acknowledge the great service he has done, and how it has pleased God to bless it with great success.'"

THE PARISH CHURCH.

The following sketch, which may be regarded as a preface to the more detailed history and description of the Parish Church of St. Lawrence was kindly furnished by the Rev. H. E. Victor, of Brighton.

From the great dearth of records relating to our parish churches, it is often a very difficult task to write their architectural history. It is indeed often not possible to do more than form a rough estimate of the date of the original building, and of subsequent alterations and additions, from a study of the different styles of architecture represented in the building itself; but even in this way it is often very difficult to arrive at any certain or definite conclusion, for in one church it frequently happens that there are visible traces of many styles of architecture, and it is often impossible to say what the original form of the building may have been, or to define what has been done in the way of alterations, save that each age seems to have set its mark on the building in some form or other. But, taking a study of the architecture of Alton Church, there is not this distraction caused by a confusion of many styles, and its features are so well defined that it seems possible to build up a guess-work history of its original form and the changes made since, which in the absence of direct record, may come very near to the truth.

There are then apparent in the church three distinct styles of architecture, and these strangely enough represent the two extremes of Gothic building, namely, early Norman, early English, and two sorts of Perpendicular or Tudor work, the flat-headed and pointed arch.

ALTON CHURCH.

St. Lawrence.—1896.

Plate IV.

From the relation these two styles now bear to each other in the structure of the building, it seems evident that the original church was a small cruciform Norman building with low central tower. The bold simplicity of the mouldings of the pillars and tower arches, which still remain, seem to point to an early date after the Norman Conquest. The capitals of the tower are supposed to have been carved by French artists, who came over early after the Conquest, and did this Church and many others. It would seem that this Norman Church must have remained untouched for several centuries, for of the many subsequent developments of architecture that followed the Norman period, the building bears no trace till that final phase of the art is reached, which in some sense marks its decay, the later form of perpendicular work, which, fast losing the beauty of its lines and the fineness of its proportions, was so soon to run to waste altogether. Just in the evening twilight of English architecture the design seems to have been formed of entirely reconstructing Alton Church, and that on a very greatly enlarged scale. These new builders first appear to have taken down the old Norman church altogether, with the exception of the central tower and its supporting piers and arches and the south wall. Then taking the line of the old south wall as the south wall of their new church, though probably lengthening it considerably eastward, they built a wide, lofty church of equal height and width from end to end externally covered with two span roofs covered with lead, afterwards altered to one large roof, but internally divided down the middle by a lofty arcade. Each division had its own low pitched timber roof, the principals resting on stone corbels. The effect of this internally was to give a church consisting of nave and south aisle both of equal length and width.

The portion of the south aisle eastward of the tower formed a chapel, of which the Piscina and Aumbry remain in good preservation. The new roof being much more lofty than that of the original church, the old Norman belfry windows come beneath it, and now open into the

E 2

church.   There are large perpendicular windows at the east
and west of both nave and aisle, the north and east walls
being pierced windows almost, but not quite square headed.
Even in the old part of the south wall these windows have
replaced whatever Norman openings there may have
been ; the only trace of Norman work left beside those already mentioned being a piscina and portions of the carved
jambs of the old south door, now built up, also remains of
Norman capitals on south wall.

Externally the new church was built of local flint and
stone groins covered with plaster ; internally the stone used
probably came from Purbeck or the Isle of Wight ; but it
seems clear that the stone of the later church differed
from that of the older one.   Probably at the same time the
church was rebuilt the tower was raised considerably in
height and surmounted by a broad spire of timber covered
with lead, rising to a height of 120 feet.   Then, either at
this time, or a later date, a peal of bells was added, and
here at once it is apparent that a curious plan was adopted
in the hanging of these bells.   The old Norman piers,
originally designed only to carry the low Norman tower,
had already been heavily taxed to carry the weight of the
heavier tower and lofty spire, and it was clearly felt unsafe
to put further strain on them by the additional weight of
the bells and their vibration when in use.   Massive oak
frames, resting on the floor of the church, were therefore
set up in each of the inside angles of the tower piers, and
these beams carry the framework on which the bells are
hung in the belfrey above.

Some oak screen work, now dividing the chancel from
the chantry, and some fine miserere stalls are all that remain
of the internal fittings of this reconstructed church, and are
shifted to present positions.

Passing on from these times through the Reformation,
and past it, Alton Church gives us a very forcible illustra-
tion of that pew and pulpit age which held such deadening
sway during the last and early portion of the present century.   When neglectful and careless of the Sacraments

UNDER
THE
BELFRY.

Plate V.

ST. LAWRENCE.—1896.

and church order, and true devotion, the popular religious idea too often seemed to find expression in a comfortable pew for the worshipper, which should command a favourable view of the pulpit, itself elevated in the chief place of honour in the church.

The annexed diagram of the internal arrangements of the church as they existed in 1815, will shew how thoroughly this debased idea of Christian worship had been carried out. The altar, neglected and almost crowded out with pews, many of which were fixed with their backs towards it, stood at the east end, almost obscured by a great gallery running right across the chancel. Close to it stood the font, moved from its proper place by the south door, the only ground for such removal seemingly being that in its lawful place it occupied space available for pews in what was considered a good position. The pulpit, then a three-decker, with an old sounding board over, stood half-way down the nave against the north wall, facing south, and centreing as towards a magnet, were pews, covering all the floor space, so arranged as to obtain the best possible view of the preacher ; while overhead a curious medley of galleries seem to have grown up in every direction where their floor beams would find a hold. And the ownership of these pews must have been fully in keeping with the seats themselves. Those in the best position seem to have been regarded as the undisputed freehold of the well-to-do, and in the obscure and uncomfortable corners the poor found, at any rate, a magnanimous recognition.

Truly God the Holy Ghost must be in a church where such dry bones could be revivified, and the old faith and purer conception of divine worship reassert their power in men's hearts.

The next step in the history is the restoration, which in the literal meaning of the word is the bringing of the church to that form and order which should more fitly direct men's thoughts to the truer conception of heavenly worship. The pews and the galleries were removed and replaced with open seats. The altar, no longer obscured,

was made the centre towards which all else was directed.
The fine Jacobean pulpit, no longer called on to fulfil three
duties at once, was carried eastward to the end of the nave
seats. The old miserere stalls, restored and enlarged by
the addition of fine carved fronts, were once more set
up in their original place in the choir. The old font was
replaced by a new one, set under the tower, instead of what
was probably the original position, near the south door. It
is to be regretted that the old font was removed and allowed
to fall to pieces.

Later on the timber work of the spire was restored and
the old lead replaced by heart-of-oak shingles.

Such in very brief outline is a history, though, to speak
more correctly, only a suggestive history of the church as a
building. There it stands, with its stamp of Norman
origin, with its signs of later development, with its scraps
and traces of beautifying fresco, side by side with remnants
of desecrating whitewash, with its walls and woodwork
pitted with Cromwell's bullets, with its fresh traces of the
love and care of a later age. There it stands, with its spire
pointing heavenward, to those who will seek its shelter,
their true home on earth, to all willing or unwilling, a
solemn and a ceaseless preacher of the presence of God
amongst us, and of that Holy Faith which alone can lead
us to the eternal city, the "building that hath foundations."

St. Lawrence Church.

The Parish
Church.
The Parish Church is situated in Church street, to the
north of the town, on somewhat high ground, about 360 feet
above the sea level. It is dedicated to St. Lawrence, and
was originally a Norman structure, and, no doubt, cruciform in shape, the square tower being in the centre. The
tower was afterwards surmounted by a steeple rising to the
height of 120 feet to the top of the weather vane.

The church is built of flints, stuccoed over, and native
stone dressings. Inside, the stone is from Purbeck or the
Isle of Wight. In the construction of the old Norman
tower the other stone is local, probably from Selborne or
Binsted.

Plate VI.

INTERIOR OF ST. LAWRENCE CHURCH, LOOKING EAST.—1867.

BEFORE RESTORATION.

The roof is in two spans, but at some period made into one wide roof externally, and is covered with lead. The spire was originally covered with lead, but in the year 1873 the old lead and boarding were removed, the defective oak timbers replaced by new, the steeple reboarded and covered with heart-of-oak shingles.

The spire was on June 24th, 1880, struck by lightning, but fortunately was not seriously injured.

There are eight Norman windows in the tower.

The arches supporting the tower are good examples of late Norman architecture and have some grotesque figures carved on the capitols, supposed to have been done by French artists who came over soon after the Conquest. The north and south transepts at some period were removed, the east and west arms only remaining, but not quite in their original condition, inasmuch as they have been widened, the outer north walls taken away and a new north aisle added. At the west end of the church and in the south wall are the remains of a capitol and commencement of an arch of considerable span, an entrance, in all probability, to the original church.

The other windows are all perpendicular, many flat-headed, and none of them belong to the original structure. There are four small Norman windows in the belfry, those looking to the east and west being intact, the north and south being closed at the time the transepts were removed. There are no remains of any ancient stained glass, but those windows containing stained glass are of recent date. The large chancel window was erected at the cost of £400, raised by public subscription, in 1870, to the memory of the late Rev. Edward James, Canon of Winchester, who was Vicar of Alton for twenty-two years. The subject of the centre light is the "Ascension of Our Lord," and "His Baptism" and "The Last Supper" are represented on the left and right. The window was manufactured by Capronnier, of Brussels. The east window of the old chancel is also filled with stained glass, the subject being "Christ healing the Sick." "It was inserted by public subscription

A.D. 1884, in grateful memory of Louis Leslie, M.D., of Amery House, who practised as a Physician in this town and neighbourhood for nearly forty years. Born Oct. 6th, 1822. Died Nov. 25th, 1883." It cost £350.

The window next to the pulpit is filled with stained glass, "To the glory of God. In memory of Martha Hutchins. Died March 25th, 1873." It represents the three Marys : St. Mary Magdalene, St. Mary B.V., St. Mary Cleophas.

The last two windows were by Messrs. Heaton, Butler and Bayne, of London.

There is also a stained glass window under the belfry to the memory of the late John Dyer and Martha his wife, and of Nancy Martha, wife of William Dyer, erected by members of the family   The subjects are, " This is my beloved Son, in Whom I am well pleased," and, " Suffer little children to come unto Me."

The roof is of oak, in the perpendicular style, with tie beams and rafters shewing ; during the restoration many bullets were taken out from the timbers. The stone corbels supporting the hammer beams are in several cases carved with heads, some of them very grotesque.

Some fine fresco paintings, dating probably from the fourteenth century, were in 1839 discovered on the walls, after having long been concealed by whitewash, and are still to be seen on one of the pillars facing the north. They are supposed to represent St. Cornelius, a bishop and a king. From the traces of colour still remaining, it would appear that the Norman arches of the tower were originally covered with frescoes.

The few encaustic tiles found during the restoration were unfortunately put in the vestry doorway, and, in consequence, are now very much worn.

The church was originally seated with old-fashioned high pews, which the congregation entered by a high step, the whole floor being on a much lower level.

Large galleries extended round the church, and one crossed the aisle in front of the communion table, with its

FRESCO PAINTINGS.—XIV CENTURY.

Plate VII.

back to the east window. One gallery was entered from the belfry.

Between each pew door in the north aisle was a small seat for the use of the inmates of the workhouse.

I find in the old Church Vestry Book that at a Vestry held 13th December, 1814, "it was resolved that a new gallery be erected in the vacant space over where the engine stands, and that seats be erected down the middle aisle."

Also in 1839–40, "a subscription was raised for cleaning and colouring the interior of the church, and the erecting of nine additional pews under the galleries in the chancel, and the oak Gothic doors and screen near the west entrance."

"Again, at a vestry held the 3rd day of August, 1843, it was considered most desirable (with a view to increasing the accommodation in the church) that all the pews be cut down to the same level; and the churchwardens are requested to take measures to carry this into effect, with a view to remove the gallery over the altar and placing it in the chancel."

At the restoration, in 1867, all the old high pews and galleries were removed, the floor raised, and a new gallery placed across the whole width of the west end of the church, and the body of the church was seated throughout with comfortable low pews.

The old font was very plain, and at the time of the restoration, in 1867, it was removed and replaced by one carved in Caen stone by the then Vicar, the Rev. O. A. Hodgson. It is octagon in shape, and the carvings on the panels represent the emblems of the Passion.

At one time, in 1814, the old font stood close to the altar rails.

There is nothing of interest to record about the altar. The communion table stands on raised steps, and at the time of the restoration the wall was faced with coloured tiles. About 1878 or 1879 a dossal was put up, and on either side curtains were hung. A super-altar was added, upon which was placed an oak cross, gilded, and two vases for flowers.

On Christmas Day, 1894, a brass cross was given to the church to replace the gilded oak cross standing on the super altar.

A design for a new reredos for the church, by Sir Arthur Blomfield, A.R.A., has been approved and adopted. It is to be of carved oak, in the perpendicular style, and will be erected as soon as the money can be raised.

The pulpit in 1814 was removed from some part to near the singing gallery. At the time of the restoration it stood somewhat to the west of the middle of the north aisle, and its character of a three-decker, as it was called, the pulpit above, the reading desk in the middle, and the clerk's desk below, was done away with. There was at that time an old conical shaped sounding board over.

The pulpit, which is of rich old oak panelling, receding behind pillars and arches, is a splendid specimen of Jacobite carving, and now stands on a stone base near the organ.

The lectern is an eagle, beautifully carved in oak, and executed by the late Rev. A. W. Deey, who was for some years curate of Alton. It stands on an oak carved pedestal. The old oak screen of open work is very antique ; it was taken from near the belfry during the restoration, and now divides the old from the present chancel, near the altar rails. The ancient oak miserere stalls are used as a part of the choir stalls.

The new carved oak choir stalls were designed by Herbert Kitchin, Esq., of Winchester, and placed in the church in 1886. They cost about £90, the money being raised by subscription. The poor box is of oak and is very old ; it is fixed on the pillar near the altar rails, and has the following inscription printed over it : " Remember the poore, and turn not thy face from any poore man, and the face of the Lord shall not be turned away from thee."— *Tobit.* iv, 7 vers. " If thou hast but little, give little ; if much, give plenteously."

As you enter by the large west entrance, the doors are of massive oak, riddled and splintered by canon balls and bullets during the battle between the Royalists

JACOBEAN PULPIT.   THE LECTERN.

and Rebels. Several bullets are also seen embedded in the stone columns of the tower.

At the west end of the church, under the gallery is a doorway, the remains of which are seen from the outside ; it was closed at the restoration.

Immediately on the left hand, on the inside of the church, is seen a holy water stoup.

Under the second window of the west end of the north wall are traces of a small doorway.

On the south wall, by the east window, there are a double piscina and aumbry, and on either side of the east window are two arched niches, in which statues at some time stood. High up in the solid stonework of the east window is carved a crozier, and opposite to it on the east aspect of the wall of the tower is carved another, exactly similar in shape and size. It has been conjectured that these croziers were held by figures carved and let into niches in the wall, and the figures being broken, the niches were filled up with plaster, and the croziers allowed to remain. But this is very uncertain.

Over the east entrance door, leading into the south-east chapel there are the letters R and H carved each on a shield in either angle of the top of the archway.

From the Alton Church Minute Book I find that on February 27th, 1829, it was " Resolved that a barrel organ be erected in the church, provided the cost of the organ and every expense incurred by its erection be paid for by a subscription, etc."

At a Vestry held June 25th, 1829, " It is resolved, That, provided a faculty be obtained for erecting the said organ in the said church, and which faculty shall contain a clause whereby the said Parish shall at all times be held harmless from all costs, charges and expenses of playing and repairing the said organ, or which may in any manner be occasioned thereby. That the said organ may and shall have finger keys thereto as well as barrels."

The organ stood in the west gallery.

At the time of the restoration, in 1867, a new organ chamber was built out by Mr. William Dyer and his sisters, on the north side of the north aisle, somewhat near the altar, under which was placed the stove and boiler to supply the heating apparatus.

The old organ was sold, and bought by the Congregationalists.

The new organ is considered one of the best in the County, and was manufactured by Messrs. Speechley and Ingram, of London, at a cost of £850. It was presented to the church in memory of the late C. M. Burnett, M.D., chiefly through the instrumentality of his son, the Rev. M. Burnett. It contains 1960 pipes, 3 manuals and 40 stops.

The organ was built in 1866; and in 1895, after nearly thirty years, it was entirely cleaned and restored, with the additions of: new pedal board, tubular pneumatics to pedal organ, tremulant to choir, voix celeste to swell, small open diapason and trumpet to great, and the front pipes decorated in gold and colours.

The church is heated by hot water pipes and lighted by gas pendants. The cost of the restoration amounted to £3553. The designs were planned by Mr. Christian, Architect to the Ecclesiastical Commissioners, White Hall Place, London.

The royal arms that were formerly put up in all churches by command—mention of which has been already made in this book—are now placed over the inner door in the south porch. The bells are hung in oak frames, supported from the ground by four massive oak posts, and are fixed quite independent of the stone walls.

I find no entry as to when the first bells were placed in the church tower, but in the Parish Vestry Book, dated 12th August, 1742, I read as follows :—

" We call this Vestry to Inform you that we are Endeavouring to Raise a New Treble Bell, In order to make Six Bells, and Intend to Raise him by subscription. But if it should so happen That There should be Two or Three Pounds wanting In the Subscription, we desire the consent of this vestry to have it allowed out of the Church Rate."

" We Likewise are a going to Cast the Great Bell, and

Plate IX.

INTERIOR OF ST. LAWRENCE CHURCH, LOOKING WEST.—1867.

BEFORE RESTORATION.

Intend to cast him to his Proper Letter, which Is F. And if it should so Happen that there should be an overplus of Mettle Left, Desires the consent of this vestry to Add It to the New Treble Bell, which Bell is Intended to Be Raised by Subscription."

"Weight of the Treble and Tennor Bells when hung up in the year 1742 :—

		Cw.		
Treble	...	8	0	25
Tennor	...	22	0	26
Fifth	...	15	1	24	Cast in the year 1754."

"April 27th, 1744. To Thos. Lister, for Casting the Great Bell. Is Weight Is 22 cw. 26. £22. 15s. 5½d."

" And on Oct. 3rd, 1785, a meeting was held at the vestry for a new rate to be made for the recasting of the six Old Bells and the additional metal for eight."

"At a vestry held 24th Oct., 1889, ' It was decided that the Bells be rehung, and that No. 7 be recast, as it is cracked, at an estimated cost of £30, by Messrs Meers and Stainbank. The money was raised by subscription.'"

" Inscription on the bells at St. Lawrence's Church :—
Treble. Thomas Janaway of London, 1803, Fecit.
2nd. Thomas Janaway, Fecit, 1785.
3rd. Thomas Janaway, Fecit, 1785.
4th. Thomas Janaway, Fecit, 1785.
5th. 'When from the earth our notes rebound
The hills and valeys echo round.'

Thomas Janaway, 1785.
6th. Thomas Janaway of Chelsea made us all, 1785.
Musica. Est. Mentio. Medicina.
7th. Thomas Janaway, Fecit, 1785.
Rev. F. Whyley, M.A., Vicar, 1890.
Recast by Mears and Stainbank.
Tenor. Rev. Dr. Thomas Balguy, Vicar.
James Dicker, Richard Palmer Baker, John Phillips,

Churchwardens.
1785. Thomas Janaway, Fecit."

Five notice boards are suspended in the belfry, giving an account of certain change ringing by the ringers, and are as follow :—

"On Friday, March 7th, 1777, was rung 5040 changes, containing 42 grandsires, in 3 hours and 28 minutes, being the most ever rung on these bells.

John Goodyer, Trible.	James Gill, second.
Wm. Gill, third.	Wm. Dyer, fourth.
John Butler, fifth.	Moses Fielder ⎫ Tenor.
	Richard Harding ⎭

"These bells were cast in 1785, and on the 15th Feby., 1789, were rung 5040 changes of Bob Major in 3 hours and 15 minutes, being the first peal completed on them.

Wm. Gill, Sen., Treble.	Jas. Gill, 2d.
Wm. Gill, Jun., 3rd.	John Dyer, 4.
Wm. Dowden, 5.	Richard Harding, 6.
John Butler, 7.	Wm. Dyer, Tenor.

Mr. T. Lee ⎫
Mr. R. Marshall ⎬ Churchwardens."
Mr. S. Dicker ⎭

"Winchester Diocesan Guild, on Thursday, Nov. 3rd, 1891, in 3 hours and 1 min. a peal of Grandsire Triples, 5040 changes, Taylor's variation.

C. Forder, Treble.	H. Withers, 2nd.
J. Ballard, 3rd.	F. Wilson, 4th.
E. Finden, 5th.	H. White, 6th.
G. Barnett, 7th.	J. Goodale, Tenor.

Conducted by H. White."

"Winchester Diocesan Guild, on Saturday, Nov. 12th, 1892, in 2 hours, 57 minutes, a peal of Grandsire Triples, 5040 changes, Holt's Ten-parte.

A. Burgess, Treble.	H. E. Withers, 2.
W. Withers, 3.	W. White, 4.
F. Finden, 5.	W. May, 6.
C. Forder, 7.	J. Goodale, 8.

Conducted by Harry E. Withers.

	Gerald Hall ⎫
Francis Whyley, Vicar.	Edward Dyer ⎬ Churchwardens."
	Wm. Curtis ⎭

"Winchester Diocesan Guild, on Monday, May 14th, 1894, in 3 hours, 3 minutes, a peal of Grandsire Triples, 5040 changes, Holt's Ten-part.

E. Bryant, Treble.	H. E. Withers, 5.
Rev. F. Whyley, 2.	G. Gasson, 6.
G. Reading, 3.	A. Burgess, 7.
W. Withers, 4.	J. Goodale, Tenor.

Conducted by Harry E. Withers.

Francis Whyley, Vicar.

Gerald Hall ⎫
Edward Dyer ⎬ Churchwardens."
William Curtis ⎭

An old wooden panelled clock face with a gilt star pointing to each of the hours, and the date 1700, is placed in the belfry, but its original position is not known. In the vestry now hangs a brass candelabra containing sixteen sconces in two tiers; it was removed from the church at the restoration. It has inscribed upon it, " Thomas Baver-stock, Gent., 1780."

In 1889 a new clock was purchased from Messrs. Benson, at an estimated cost of £250, to strike the West-minster chimes. The money was raised by voluntary con-tributions.

The church plate consists of :—

1. Flagon, silver gilt, inscribed—

" In Gloriam Dei pro nobis Crucifixi,
usumque Ejus apud Altoniensis Altaris
Lagenam hanc unà cum patinâ deauratâ
Pallâque heteroniallâ, omnibus Dominicis
Festisque diebus,
Sacræ mensæ rite insterneuda
Testamento dicavit
Gulielmus Turner
ex hâc paræciâ generosus
Anno D n̄i
1721."

Translation.

" To the glory of God, crucified for us, and for His use at the Altar of Alton, this flagon, together with a gilt paten and a woolen cloth, to be duly used for covering the Holy Table on all Sundays and Festival Days, left by will, William Turner, a gentle-man of this Parish, A.D. 1721."

2. Flagon, silver, inscribed—

"The gift of Matthew Hawkins, as a legacy of his eldest son Matthew; born of Mary his wife, daughter of Lawrence Geale, Jan. 1st, 1684, who died in London, Aprill ye 29th, and was buried in this Church May 1st, 1711."

3. Alms dish, silver gilt, inscribed with coat of arms and I. H. S. in centre.

> "Deo Salvatori Sacram
> In usum Altaris Altoniensis
> Dedit Edvardus Fisher
> ex hoc oppido generosus, 1722."

Translation.

"Sacred to God our Saviour for use of the Altar of Alton. Given by Edward Fisher, a gentleman of this Town, 1722."

4. Alms dish, silver, no inscription, but I. H. S. in centre.

5. Cup, large, silver gilt. No inscription.

6. Cup, small, silver gilt, inscribed—

> "Deo Salvatori Sacram
> In usum Altaris Altoniensis
> Dedit Elizab^h Baker
> ex hoc oppido generosa
> 1818."

Translation.

"Sacred to God our Saviour, for use of the Altar of Alton. Given by Elizabeth Baker, a Gentlewoman of the Town, 1818."

7. Paten, large, silver gilt. No inscription, but I. H. S. in centre.

8. Paten, small, silver. I. H. S. in front centre. Inscribed on back.

> "Presented by William Dyer
> September, 1859,
> in the 14th year of his serving the office of
> Churchwarden in the Parish of Alton."

There are several old brasses.

"Of your charity, pray for the soul of Richard Clarke, which deceased the xvi day of April, in the year of our Lord God MIIIILXXXV; and for the soul of Margery, his daughter, late the wife of Richard Fylder, the which deceased the xxv day of April, in the year of our Lord God, MVXXXIIII.

"On whose soul Jesu have mercy. Amen."

"Here under lyeth Xopher Walaston, who sometime was groom of y⁰ chamber, and one of the Yostregere unto y⁰ late Kinges and Quenes of famous memorye, Henry y⁰ VIII, Edwarde y⁰ VI, Philip and Mary, and to our sovayn Ladye Elizabethe, y⁰ Quen's Majesty, that now is, which Xopher departed thee miserable worlde the xvi daye of y⁰ monght of Janvari Ano. Dom. MVLXIII."

Note.—Yostregere.[1] "This word, with the initial Y, does not seem to have been noticed elsewhere. It is usually spelt Austringer, also astr—, ostr—." "They be calde Ostregeris that kepe Goshawkys," a keeper of Goshawks. 1486, B. K., St. Albans. "1670-1717. We usually call a Faulkoner who keeps that kind of Hawks an Ostringer."

"Enter a gentle astringer."—*Shakespeare.* "All's well that ends well."
Act V, Scene I.

A third is an old brass standing figure of a lady, under which is a separate brass, upon which is inscribed—

"Memento Mori,

Here lyeth the body of Elizabeth Geale, who departed this life the xxvth day of Maie, Anno Domini, 1638.

Her desire of her parents was as followeth :

Deare parents weep not, I live and have abode In blisse,

Enjoying heaven, posterity and God.

Vivo fruor tandem veris (ne flete parentes),

Deliciis, Cælo, posteritate, Deo."

There is also a very small brass of three figures, probably nuns, but no inscription.

On the column near the altar rails is an old brass with the following :—

"In the family vault, near this Pillar, Lyeth the Body of Thomas Pinke, Sen., who died October the 22nd, 1713.

Also of Ann, his wife, who died Feb. 17th, 1720.

Also of Thomas Pinke, his son, who died May the 19th, 1765.

Also of Elizabeth, his wife, who died June the 24th, 1753.

With three small children of 'Thoˢ. and Elizᵗʰ."

Over the small entrance door is a tablet, with a small brass, inscribed as follows, and it is a strange coincidence that a duplicate brass is found in the vestry :—

[1] Extracts from the *New English Dictionary on Historical Principles*, by J. K. Murray.

F

" Here lyeth yᵉ Body of Robert Fry (late Hedd Bailliffe of this Towne), who died yᵉ twelveth day of Novembʳ., and was buried yᵉ fiveteenth day of yᵉ same, An. D-ni, 1620.

Villicationis Rationem Redidi."

There is also an old brass in the vestry.

"In humble Hope of a Blessed Resurrection.

Here are deposited the remains of Mr. John Pinke, of this Town. He departed this life the 17th September, 1772, aged 65 years."

A small brass plate is placed on the first column on the left as you enter by the large doors.

"Thomas Clement, Esq., of Alton, died Oct. 13th, 1826, aged 71.   Jane, his wife, daughter of Benjamin White, Esq., of South Lambeth, died January 3rd, 1831, aged 75.

Their remains are deposited in the vault on the south side of this pier."

On the second column is a more recent brass, "in memory of Joseph and Emma Thompson and their children ; erected by the only surviving daughter, Elizabeth Mary Thompson, A.D., 1876."

Also a brass tablet, a facsimile to the one placed on a column in the nave of Winchester Cathedral to the memory of Colonel Richard Bolles, who was killed during the Civil War, in Alton Church, in defending the town.

"A Memoriall

For this Renowned Martialist, Richard Boles, of ye
Right Worshipfull Family of the Bolses in
Linckhornesheire, Colonel of a Ridgment of Foot
of 1300, who for His Gratious King Charles ye First
did wounders att the Battell of Edgehill.   His last
action, to omitt all others, was at Alton, in this
County of Soughthampton, was sirprised by five or
six thousand of the Rebells, which caused him there
quartered, to fly to the church with neare Fourscore
of his men, who there Fought them six or seven
Houers, and there the Rebell Breaking in upon him,
he slew with his sword six or seven of them and
then he was slayne himselfe, with sixty of his men about him."

1641.

"His Gracious Soveraigne, hearing of his death, gave him his
high comendation in ye pationate expression,
'Bring me a moorning Scarffe, I have lost one of
the best comanders in this Kingdome,'
Alton will tell you of that famous fight
Which yᵉ man made and bade this World Goodnight.
His Verteous Life fear'd not Mortalyty
His Body must, his Vertues cannot die,
Because his Bloud was there so Nobly spent.
This is his Tombe, that Church his monument."
    Ricardus Boleo, Wiltoniensis in Art. Mag.
        Composuit Prosuitque Dolens
            An. Dmi, 1689."[1]

A somewhat recent brass is erected on the pillar by the
Altar rails, written in Latin, to the memory of Canon
James:—

"In honorem Dei et in piam memoriam
    Eduardi James A. M.
    hujus Ecclesiæ xxii Annos Vicarii
    fenestram hanc orientalem posuerunt
        Vidua, Liberi, Amici
    Decessit sexto die Aprilis
        M D C C C L I V
    Cum Illo mansurus quam
    Ascendentem in tabulæ vides."

Translation.

"To the honour of God, and in pious memory of Edward
James, A.M., 22 years Vicar of this Church, this East Window
was erected by his widow, children and friends. He died on the
6th day of April, 1854, about to rest with Him Whom you see
ascending in the picture."

Another near it, also in Latin, runs thus:—

"M. S.   Theologorum
    Thomæ Balguy, S.T.P. Archidiaconi
    Winton. et hujus ecclesiæ Vicarii
    ab A. S. MDCCLXXI ad—xcv; et
    Thomæ Rennell, S.T.P., eccles. Cathedralis
    Decani, necnon hujus Vicarii ad A. S.

[1] Composed and erected by R. Boles, mourning.

F 2

MDCCXCV ad CXIV ;
Quorum hic sacras literas raro ingenii
Accumine, Ille seravi in docendo gravitate,
Uterque vero piâ eloquentiâ
Veritatis Catholica defensor strenuus
Diligenter ac fideliter excoluit.
  Ponii curavit Edwardus James
  A. V. Vicarius.
    MDCCCXLVI."

Translation.

"Sacred to the memory of the Divines, Thomas Balguy, S.T.P., Archdeacon of Winchester and Vicar of this Church from A.D. 1771 to 1795; and Thomas Rennell, S.T.P., Dean of the Cathedral and also Vicar of this Church from A.D. 1795 to 1814, of whom the one diligently and faithfully cultivated Theology with rare acumen and ability ; the other with sweet gravity in teaching, whilst each with pious eloquence was a strenuous defender of the Catholic truth.

 Edward James, M.A., Vicar, caused this to be erected,
    1846."

A new brass tablet has recently been erected,

"In memory of William Bruce Brand, Major 93 Highlanders, who died at Aldershot 31st March, 1890, aged 40 years. Erected by his Brother Officers."

There are no monuments in the church, but numerous marble tablets against the walls, but none of any great interest.

On the south wall are found the following tablets :—

"Sacred to the memory of Stephen Lee, who died the 12th of June, 1782, aged 65 years. Also Mary, the daughter of Stephen and Mary Lee, who died the 25th of May, 1768, aged 12 years. Also of Mary, Relict of the above named Stephen Lee, who died August 6th, 1819, aged 90 years. Also Thomas, son of the above named Stephen and Mary Lee, who died May 15th, 1844, aged 87 years."

"Sacred to the memory of William Lee, Esq., of Anstey House, obiit 21st January, 1814, aged 55 years. This tablet was erected by his widow to record the virtues of a man who was truly exemplary in all the duties of life. Ann, wife of the above named William Lee, died 6th of September, 1844, aged 80 years."

"In affectionate remembrance of James Snelling, who died December 7th, 1838, aged 81 years. Also of his wife Mary and his daughter Maria."

"In memory of a beloved husband, Henry Snelling, born May 14th, 1802, died December 24th, 1864. Also of Henry Steele and William, his sons, and Susan his wife."

"In memory of William Exall, Esq., also of Jane, his wife, of Amery House, near this Church, and formerly of Welbeck Street, London. The former died on April 28th, 1843, aged 84 years, and the latter died on December 20th, 1845, aged 86 years. 'Looking for the Resurrection of the dead and the life of the world to come.'"

A tribute of filial piety to the memory of the best of parents, Martha Baverstock, died 1st January, 1781, aged 75 years. Thomas Baverstock, died 2nd January, 1781, aged 80 years. 'They were lovely and pleasant in their lives, and in their death they were not divided.'"

"In memory of William Baker, who died July 4th, 1726, aged 42 years. Also of Elizabeth his wife, William their son, and Mary his wife. Also of another son, Richard, and Elizabeth his wife, and of Richard, son of William and Mary, and Mary his wife."

Over the vestry door, on the south wall, is a tablet,—

"To the memory of Barbara, widow of the late Reverend John White, Vicar of Blackburn, who died November the 21st, 1784, and lies buried within the communion rails of that church, where a monument is fixed. She died April the 19th, 1802 in the sixty-eighth year of her age."

"In memory of Jane, the beloved wife of William Gunner, of Will Hall, in this Parish, who died April 21st, 1840, aged 37 years, also of Mary Hannah, beloved wife of William Gunner, who died August 3rd, 1855, aged 38 years. Also of William Gunner, who died March 29th, 1869, aged 68 years, and was buried in the cemetry."

Over the small eastern entrance door is a tablet,—

"Sacred to the memory of William Parker Terry, Esq., youngest son of Michael Terry, Esq., of Dummer house in this

County. Proprietor of the Rectorial tithes of this Parish. He was a sincere Christian, a kind master, benevolent to the poor and most deservedly respected by all who knew him. He married Rebecca, daughter of Benjamin White, Esq., of Selborne. He departed this life July 27th, 1816, aged 62, and was buried in this chancel."

On the north wall is a marble tablet,—

"Sacred to the memory of Richard Marshall, who died November 7th, 1843, in the 62nd year of his age." And

"In affectionate memory also of his cousin, Martha Hutchins, who died March 25th, 1873, aged 84 years."

Within the altar rails is a tablet,—

"In memory of Lawrence Hawkins, who died 26th Sept., 1732, and other members of his family. They were all buried in a vault under the western gallery."

In the gallery, against the west wall, are the following tablets :—The first represents a coat of arms at the top, and three small urns under. On the centre urn is " J.B.H., died April 11th, 1767, aged 27." On the left, " E. H., died May 10th, 1765, aged 17." And on the right, " F. H., died May 30th, 1767, aged 27."

"Sacred to the memory of John Butler Harrison, of Amery, in this Parish, Esq., and his two beloved wives. He married in July, 1764, Elizabeth, daughter of the Rev. John Ballard, D.D., and in August, 1766, Frances, daughter of Mr. Robert Ballard, Merchant, Southton. Their many and amiable virtues truth must acknowledge. Friendship will ever lament that they are now no more."

"Sacred to the memory of Eliza, daughter of John and Mary Andrews, who died the 28th of August, 1822, aged 13 years. Also of Jesse Silvester, son of the above, who died in his infancy ; both of which are buried in the vault within the yew tree fence in this churchyard. Also Sarah Hannah, born Sept. 23rd, 1818, died Feb. 9th, 1836."

"To the memory of Mary, the beloved wife of Mr. William Haslam, of Greenwich, in Kent, Gentleman, whose mortal remains are buried in this Church. She was given to him 16th of October, 1819, and died in this Parish on the 6th of the same month, 1822, in the 27th year of her age.

> Sweet spirit, who in loveliest mortal form,
> Did'st win and wean one from the world and charm
> My heart, my nature, every thought of mine,
> To seek its origin or end in thine—
> Who, mortal, were to me the source and test
> Of all that dignified or truly blest
> Man's mortal nature! Deign to guard me still!
> Now mould me, Mary, to thy heavenly will."

All the old tombstones found in the church at the time of the restoration were placed outside the church porch and vestry. On one, near the belfry, is inscribed, " Here lieth the bodies of Captaine Thomas Geale and Barbara, his former wife, which Thomas was also one of the Justices of the Peace for this Countie, and founder of ye Alms House in Aulton. He deceased August 24th, 1657."

Below this is a broken fragment, " Here lyeth also the body of Benjamin Geale, Gen^t."

There is very little of interest to be found engraved on the tombstones in the churchyard. The following seems the only one worth quoting :—

" In memory of John Ride, who died Oct. 1st, 1844, aged 68. Also Mary, wife of Willm. Pain (and sister of the above) who died Sept. 13th, 1845, aged 67 years.

> Praises on tombs are oft times vainly spent,
> Good deeds are the best monuments ! "

Mention should be made of the very handsome old wrought iron work over the south-east main entrance gates to the churchyard. It is probably Jacobean work, and between 200 and 300 years old.

A cannon ball was found in 1840 in the churchyard, and is preserved in the Curtis Museum.

Engraved on one piece of the lead covering the roof on

the south side, at the west end of the church, is the date 1776 A.D., and on the north aspect :—

> The Rev. Mr. Smith, Vicar.
> J^{no}. Gunner,
> Go^{e}. Tempel,
> Thos. Haslar,
> Churchwardens, 1758.

The early Matin bell used always to be rung at 5 in the summer and 6 in the winter, but was discontinued in March, 1880. The curfew is still regularly rung every evening at 8 o'clock.

THE VICARS OF ALTON.

Vicars of Alton.

The following is a list of some of the Vicars of Alton that I have come across in my researches, also notes of interest connected with the Parish :—

1161.

TURSTIN.—" From 1161 to 1170 Richard Turstin appears to have been the Sheriff and also Parson of Alton and Colmer, and was presented to these livings, no doubt, by Hide Abbey (Hen II reign)." [1]

1200.

HUGH.—" In the charters of Selborne Priory in two deeds, the name of Hugh the Chaplain of Aweltun is mentioned ; in one he wrote the deed, and in the other he appears as a witness." [2]

1250.

PETER DE RYEVAL.—" Rector of the Church of Alton." [3]

1305.

PETER LE TAVENER.—" Licence by Bp. Henry Woodlock to demise the churches of Aulton and Leckford to farms for the space of five years, 38. Letters directed to Sir W. de Saunsford, Proctor or Commissary of the Archdeacon of Winchester, to release the sentence of prohibition read in the Parish Church of Aweltun, 65. Probate of the will of Sir R., Rector of the Church of Aulton, deceased 102 *b*. Mandate directed to the Dean of Aulton, at the instance of the vicar there, against the bailiff

---

[1] Woodward and Wilks' *History of Hants*, p. 308.
[2] Extracts from *Charters of Selborne Priory*, p. 1.
[3] Extracts from *Annals of Waverley*, by Rev. C. Kerry, p. 54.

of the Abbot of Hyde. for carrying away the oblations, etc., belonging to the said Vicarage, 139 *b*. Letters of Henry, Bishop of Winchester, to the Vicar of Aulton, or mandate to permit the Chaplain to celebrate in the said church for the soul of his predecessor, and to restore the psaltery, etc., 146. The same to the Abbot of Hyde for the ordination and augmentation of the portion of the Vicar of the Church of Aulton, 164. Proclamation upon the clearing of Peter le Taverner of Aulton, clerk, of the death of four foreign merchants in the house of the said Peter at Aulton, 168 and 168 *b*. Commission to receive the proof of innocence_{clearing} of Peter le Taverner of Aulton, 171. Ordination to the vicarage of Aulton. Given at Southwark the 5th of the month of November, 1312, 172*b*, 173. Testamentary letters of Peter le Taverner upon his clearing [from guilt], 174. Letters of the Bishop of Winchester to Sir R. about the same, and of the things, possessions and goods to be restored to the said Peter, 175*b*. Mandate to induct the Abbot and Convent of Hyde in corporal possession of the Church of Aulton, appropriated to them, 12. Institution to the vicarage of Aulton, at the presentation of the Abbot and convent of Hyde, 156." [1]

THOMAS DE BECFORDE.—" Institution by Bp. John de Sandale to the Vicarage of the Church of Aulton, at the presentation of the Abbot and Convent of Hyde, 46 *b*." [1] . . . . . "Controversy between Stephen de Claro Monte, Rector of the Church of Bynteworth, and Thomas de Bekford, Vicar of the Parish Church of Aulton, upon the right and possession of the moiety of the tithes of lambs, to wit, of milk, wool, and cheese, of the animals of the inhabitants of the hamlet or manor which John de Thudder now inhabits, within the bounds and limits of the Parish Church of Aulton, etc. And the ordinance of John, Bishop of Winchester, upon the said tithes, 15 *b*. The ordinance of the submission of the Rector of Bynteworth and Vicar of Aulton, upon the right, etc., of the said tithes, 18 *b*.

1818.

---

[1] Egerton MS., 2031-34. British Museum.

Monition against the parishioners of Aulton that they desist from their errors, to wit, in moving the images of St. Lawrence the Martyr, in whose honor the Church there is dedicated, from the high altar, where of approved custom it ought to be, to another place, 51 *b*. Premunition to be present at the publication of the sentences to be made at Aulton. Inhibition that nobody .... shall presume to exercise "luctus," fairs, or other marts in the churches or cemeteries of the Diocese of Winchester, and especially in the church or cemetery of the Church of Aulton, or to be present at the same, 51 *b*. Sentence against the parishioners of Aulton for infringing the liberties of the church, 52. Submission of the parishioners of Aulton. Institution to the vicarage of Aulton at the presentation of the Abbot and Convent of Hyde, 122." [1]

1333.
"License granted by Bp. Adam Orlton to William Trenchaunt to celebrate Divine Service in the oratory of his house in the parish of Aulton." [1]

1346.
"Collation to the Vicarage of Aulton made by apostolic authority to the provisor, 38. License granted to let to farm the fruits of the church, to the Vicar of Aulton and Thomas Warner, layman, 95. Institution to the Vicarage by Bp. Wm. Edingdon at the presentation of the Abbot and Convent of Hyde." [1]

1370.
JOHN DE MALTEBY, Vicar of Aultone, attended Bp. Wm. of Wykeham at Highclere, 21 Sept., 1370. [2]

1378.
WILLIAM NEWETONE, Rector of West Deane, Wilts, instituted to Vicarage of Aultone, on exchange with John de Malteby, under commission to Ralph, Bp. of Sarum. [2]

1392
JOHN NEWPORT, instituted 10th April, 1392. Patrons, Abbot and Convent of Hyde. [2]

1404.
"Institution to the Vicarage of Aulton by Cardinal Beaufort, 4 *b*. The same on account of exchange with the Church of Hursley, 90 *b*." [1]

[1] Egerton MS., 2031-34. British Museum.
[2] *Wykeham's Register*, vol. i; ed. T. F. Kirby, M.A.

"Institution to the Vicarage of the Church of Aulton   1447.
by Bp. Waynflete at the presentation of the Abbot, &c., of
Hyde. Exchange of the Churches of Alton and Utilcote
in the diocese of Worcester. 145^b." [1].

WILLIAM CALEY.—"Clericus, 19 Sept., 1 and 2 Philip   1554.
and Mary." [1]

JOHN KINGTON.—"Clericus, 23 April, 20 Elizth." [2]   1578.

JOHN BARLOWE.—"Clericus, 9 Feb., 24 Elizth." [2]   1582.

JOHN HUGHES.—"Clericus, 9 Dec., 44 Elizth." [2]   1601.

WILLIAM TINDALL.—"Clericus, 10 Sept., 11 James I." [2]   1613.

March 26, 1635.—"Memoranda by Archbp. Laud in
the nature of instructions to his Vicar-General upon his
approaching visitations. In the diocese of Winchester
particular attention was to be given to Mr. Tyndall, Vicar
of Alton; the archbp. had heard that he curtailed the
Common Prayer at his pleasure." [3]

JOHN CARRILL.—"Incumbent put in by Parliament." [4]   1658.

"On consideration of the humble petition of the Inhabitants of Alton in the County of Southampton shewing
that Alton aforesaid is a Markett Towne consisting of 2000
souls and upwards and that the liveing there is a Vicarage
haveing two Chappells annexed to it the profitts of all
which (with an Augmentation of twenty-five pounds per
Ann. amounts to but one hundred and one pounds by the
yeare to discharge the three cures out of which fiftene
pounds per ann. is alsoe allowed to Mr. John Carill the
present Incumbent dureing his life. As alsoe of a Certificate endorsed upon the said peticōn And to the intent that
over and above the provision for the said Chappelrys the
Minister of Alton aforesaid may bee competently provided
for and those inconveniences sett forth in ye said petition

---

[1] Egerton MS., 2031-34. British Museum.
[2] Composition Books, 1536-1660. British Museum.
[3] State Papers, Vol. 285, No. 38, p. 601-2.
[4] Augmentation of Church Lands, Vol. 977, p. 142. Lambeth Palace Library.

bee the better prevented by encouraging a godlye and able
minister to settle and reside there Ordered by his Highnesse
the Lord Protector and the Councell that it be recommended to the Trustees for maintenance of a minister to
take an effectual Course that a further augmentation of
sixty pounds per ann. over and above the said former
augmentation of twenty-five pounds per ann. bee further
setled on ye minister of Alton aforesaid and that the same
bee duely paid from time to time to such Minister
accordingly.

Hen. Scobell, Clerk

Thursday, 30 September, 1658,   of the Councell.
  at the Councell at Whitehall."

[" In Vol. 995, fo. 523, it is stated that the said Mr.
Caryll was disabled by Lunacy to discharge the duty of
Minister of Alton."]

1660.   HENRIE BUTLER, "Clerc, seems to have combined the
functions of minister and clarke, 23 Nov. Dean and
Chapter of Winchester." [1]

1671.   SAMUEL WOODFORD, D.D., "Vicar of Alton with Binsted and Kingsley, though he seems to have lived at
Hartley Maudit." [2]

1696.   THOMAS MATTHEWS.—"5 March. The King. We
incidently glean he was still Vicar in Dec., 1736." [2]

1741.   GRIMSHAW SMITH, " as Vicar of Alton takes charge of
the Registers. He is buried in August, 1766." [1]

1766.   JAMES DENNISON "is Curate in charge—he then be-
comes Curate of Harteley Maudytt, and in 1780 of
Binsted:" [1]

1767.   DR. PHILIP WALTON—Vicar.[1]

1771.   DR. BALGUYS—Vicar.[1]

1795.   THOMAS RENNELL, D.D., "Vicar of Alton and Master of
the Temple in London. In 1807 he signs as Dean of the

---

[1] Parish Registers.
[2] *Hampshire Notes and Queries*, Vol. vi ; and *Institution Books*, Series B, Vol. vi.

Cathedral Church of Winchester, Master of the Temple in London, and Vicar of Alton."[1]

From 1808 to 1816 there appears to have been several Curates acting as such, and signing themselves "Curate and Minister," "Minister," or "Officiating Minister."

E. POULTER—signs at rare intervals, and only once incidentally calls himself Vicar in 1825.[1]   1816.

JOHN BANNISTER—in charge.[1]   1827.

EDWARD JAMES—who in 1834 is called Prebendary of Winchester.[1]   1832.

H. P. BROCK—in charge.[1]   1853.

THOMAS WOODROOFE—Vicar.[1]   1855.

OCTAVIUS A. HODGSON—Vicar.[1]   1863.

WILLIAM DURST—Vicar.[1]   1874.

FRANCIS WHYLEY—Vicar.[1]   1881.

PARISH REGISTERS.

The earliest volume of the Registers dates from 1615 and ends in 1711. It commences with Baptisms, but the entries for some few years were kept in a most irregular manner, there being only one or two entries made—none in 1618 or 1628. In 1630 the entries increase considerably, there being as many as twenty-nine; in 1631, seventy-one. During the years 1638-39-40 no Registers were kept of either Births, Marriages, or Deaths. This was accounted for by the Civil War between the King and Parliament; the same may be said of 1643, 1644, and 1649.   1615 Baptisms.

In 1653 the following memorandum is found :—" A true register of the names of All Children borne in the towne e pish of Alton since the 29th of September in the year of Our lord god 1653 kept by Rob[t]. Bushell, appoynted thereunto by order of Authoritee." The Baptisms continue to be regularly entered from now to the end of the volume, 1710.

The second volume dates from 1711 to 1765, and contains Baptisms, Burials, and Marriages, and are regularly kept.

[1] Parish Registers.

An entry is made the 9th June, 1712, that " Mary, Ann, Elizabeth and Sarah daughters of John and Mary Stephens, Quakers by ye Mother's side, all baptized together."

" 1714 Abraham Westbrook an Adult Quaker bap^d. Dec. 18th," and " Priscilla Bullpit born of Quaker Parents Bap^d. about ye time."

The third volume contains only Baptisms and Burials, which dates from 1760 to 1812. Entries irregular from 1760 to 1770, whole months missed out, and there seems confusion sometimes as to the year, as if what entries there are are transcripts.

" 1808. A private of ye Coldstream Regiment of Guards, their children baptized."

1629.
Marriages.

The first Marriages recorded commence in 1629, and are entered as follows :—

" Henrie Clark and Maria Johnson were marryed 8 June."

" John Mortimer and Katharina Tomalin were marryed 22 June."

The entries were few in number each year till 1638.

During 1638–39 and 40 no entries are made.

In 1641 they commence again.

" Willia Wake and Martha Neave were married the 25th of May."

" Robert Pallard and Ann Bun were married the 22nd June."

From 1642 till 1653 no entries exist.

" Memorand, that the first day of Octob., 1653, was presented unto me Robert Bushell of this towne of Alton to be sworne Regester, being thereunto elected by the Maior etc. of the prish for that purpose met together according to the act of Pliament in that case made and provided for the the registrance of All Mariages, Births and Burrials wh. should happen to be in the s^d. towne, wh. s^d. Regester was sworne to the Office afores^d. the day and year above s^d. by me,
                                        Edw. Heighes."

At the end of the 1st volume of registers there is a list of the signatures of those who elected Robert Bushell, but there is no indication as to which was " Maior."

"A register of the names of all such psons as have been married in this towne and prish of Alton since the 29th of September anno 1653, with the manner of p.ceding thereunto in relacon to the order sett foorth and commanded by authoritie."

The entries are now more elaborate ; from 1654 to 1657 they were married by a Justice of the Peace, and their banns were published on three succeeding Sundays in Church, or three following market days in the market place.

" That there was a marriage intended to be made between John Bullock, the son of Robt. Bullock of this towne of Alton, and Elizabeth Westbrooke, daughter of Thomas Westbrooke of the sayd Alton, was published the first time upon the first day of March Anno domini 1654. The second time upon the 12th of the same ; and the third and last time upon the 19th of March aforesaid, which being done the marriage was solemnized the 28th of the same month in the p-sence of Mr. Heighes one of the iustices of the peace for this Countie and others."

" A marriage intended to be made between Thomas Bullock sonn of Robt. Bullock of this towne of Alton and Ann Sylvester, daughter of Maria Sylvester of Tystwad, widdow, was first published upon the 12th day of March. The second day upon the 19th of the same, and the third and last upon the 26th. The marriage was solemnized before Mr. Hooke one of the Justices of the peace for this Countie and some others upon the 13th daye of Aprill."

" Publicacon of a marriage intended to be made between Thomas Lee of the pish of Nuchelyn in this County of South and Elizabeth Nicolson sometimes the wife of Willm. Nicholson borne in this towne of Alton was first made August the 20th ; the second time Aug. the 27th ; the last time September the first. The marriage was solemnized before Mr. Riggs Magertes October the 31st.

" That there was a marriage intended to be made between Andrew Pile of this towne of Alton Appothecare, the sonne of Richard Pyle of Ash in the Countie of Surrey, Yeoman, and Dorothy Green daughter of William Green sometimes of Weeke of the pish of Bynsteed in this Countie of South, but now deceased, have been published by me three severall Sabbath days accordinge to the command of Authoritie, which being done they were married februarii the 12th by Mr. Gale one of the justices of the peace for this Countie then being present."

"Edward Heather of the Town of Alton, the sonne of John Heather of East Woordha in this Countie of South Yeoman and Ann Steed the daughter of Nicholas Steed of the town and pish of Hynchnux in this Countie of South Yeoman were married by Mr. Heyghes one of the Justices of the peace for this Countie upon the fourth day of June ; the intent of their marriage having been published three several market days in the market place of Alton aforesayd to witt upon May the 6th the 13th and the 20th and noe excepcon against it. These were present at the marriage, Tho⁸. Steed, Robᵗ. Smyth.

It appears that now and then people belonging to other parishes would bring a certificate stating that the banns had been duly published in their own churches, but wished to be married by the Justice of the Peace residing in Alton.

Some of these parishes were Holybourne, Froyle—spelt Froill, Froyell, or Froell,—Bynsteed, Crundall, Bishop's Sutton, Basingstoke, Selborne, Newton, East Tisted, Headley, Froxfield, Empshot, Petersfield, Bentworth, Medstead, and Odiham.

In the year 1657 some of the marriages were solemnized by the Clergy, and we find a note made in 1660 that "Since this Register was dellivered to Mr. Henrye Butler of Alton, Clarke, are thus as followeth."

"Nicholas Allam was married to his second wiffe at the pishe Church where his wiffe was borne the 25th February 1660."

"John Coop and Mary Collens married the 27 daye of Novem."

The entries after this are very simple, only giving their names, and occasionally the name of the parish.

These entries end in 1710.

The second volume dates from 1711 to 1765, and the entries appear to have been kept regularly, but few in number, till 1753.

The fourth volume, or third of Marriages, contains a register of Marriages at Alton in the County of Southampton from 1754 to 1785, and for " Holyborn being extra parochial."

"Martin Knyck Van Microp of the Parish of Saint Botolph Bishopsgate, London, Bachelor, and Martha Bates of Alton in the County of Southampton, Spinster, were married in this Church by Licence (from ye Arch Bishop of Canterbury) this fourteenth Day of May in the year of our Lord one thousand seven Hundred and fifty four.

By me Grimshaw Smith, Vicar of Alton.

This marriage was solemnized between us

        Martin Knyckvan Microp.

        Martha Bates now Microp.

in the presence of Thos Bates—Elizth Bates."

" Memorandum.—Holy-Born (this spelling is exceptional) is a chapelry belonging to Alton where there not being Divine Service performed every Sunday by ye Vicar of Alton, it is deemed Extra-parochial by a clause in ye late Act of Parliament. Therefore Banns were published and ye Marriage solemnized at Alton [1754–58]."

"William Penton of ye Chapelry of Holyborn in ye County of Southampton, and Mary Knight of ye same Chappelry and County were married in this Church by Banns Duly published this thirtieth Day of September in ye year 1754.

    By me G. Smith, Vicar.   William Penton.

This Marriage was solemnized between us

                    The mark + of Mary

                    Penton late Knight.

In the presence of us is mark + of John Knight

                    of Shalden.

    Wm Trimmer."

In 1809 Holybourne is still spoken of as a chapelry, an appendage of this parish.

G

In 1818 The "Tything of Neatham" is spoken of as appendant to the Parish of Alton.

The last entry in which the Chapelry of Holybourne is mentioned appears to be 8th May, 1821.

"1754, June.   Entry of the marriage of Edward Bentham, D.D. one of the Canons of Christchurch Oxford, he was later Regius Professor of Divinity at Oxford and elder brother of the more famous James Bentham writer on Eccl : Archiology."

"1776.   5 Soldiers married 1 of 'The Queens Royal Reg^t' and 4 of the '2nd Reg^t.'"

"1781.   2 Soldiers married 1 of the 'Northumberland Militia' and 1 of the 'West Kentish Militia.'"

The Registers appear to have been kept regularly from now and in 1809 a new Registration commences.

"The Register Book for Marriages in all Parish Churches and Chapels conformable to the Act of Parliament in the 26th year of King George II, entitled 'An Act for the better preventing of Clandestine Marriages.'"

1616. Burials.

Burials.—One entry is made in 1616 and one in 1622. From 1629 to 1637 the entries are regular, but from 1638 to 1640 they cease ; they continue in 1641–42, but from 1643 to the end of 1652 there is a complete blank.

Two pages are given up to the Matthews family, apparently transcripts of the entries relating to the then Vicars family.   The entries range from 1644—1690.

They begin again in 1653, and a memorand is made as follows :—

"A true register of the names of all those that have been buried in the pish of Alton, since the 29th of September in the year of o^r lord god one thousand six hundred fifty and three, kept by mee Robert Bushell appoynted thereunto by authoritie."

1660 an entry is made, "Burialls since the Regist^r deliv'ed to Mr. Henry Butler of Alton Clarke, as followeth."

The visitation of the Plague seems to have been very

severe in Alton about the same time, or shortly before it reached London. The first entry is " Goody Browne and three of her dafters died of the sickness and Plague in July Anno domino 1665 at Alton in Browne's haus." Then follows a page and a half of irregular entries, from the nature of which the illness appears to have been of a virulent character, many of a family being buried in quick succession. Among others the " Ostler of the Swan " is mentioned as a victim. The illness lingered on until the opening of the new year.

Feb. 28th, 1701, an entry is made of Benjn. Gates, a Quaker child, buried. Also of Sarah Godfrey, Quaker, buried in yᵉ Quakers' burying place. The burials are carried on regularly in this volume till the end of 1710.

The 2nd Register Book dates from 1711 to 1765, and the entries are kept regularly. An entry is made in 1721 as follows :—

"William Turner who by his Will bequeath'd fifty pounds to purchase a Gilt Flagon, Paten, and a Velvet Carpet for the Altar was Burᵈ. Oct. 10th, 1721."

In 1722 the burials are entered as before, but followed by the words, Affid. Recᵈ.

" Edward Fisher who gave several noble Benefactions to yᵉ Church and Poor of yᵉ Parish of Alton, was Buried yᵉ 25th May. Affid. Recᵈ. yᵉ 30th, 1723."

Each year ending April is now signed as follows :—
" Apⁱˡ. 20th, 1723.
      Allowed of this amount of buryalls by us
                  Simson Stuart
                  Robert Kercher."

" In 1730, Affid. Recd. in due Time for Joan Chandler, Robᵗ. Norris and Moses Neave, Quakers.
                  J. Sumner, Cur. of Alton."

" John Butler Esq. of Amery High Sheriff of yᵉ County died May, 1736."

" Elizabeth Matthew the Vicars Sister buried Dec. 20th, 1736."

The entries continue regularly till 1758. In 1759 there are only a few scattered entries and then cease altogether in this book.

The 3rd Volume contains only Baptisms and Burials, which date from 1760 to 1812.

1794, a Suffolk militia man buried.

At the end of the year 1804 the following entry is made in red ink :—" 17 Marriages, 65 Baptisms and 44 Burials. This return made to the Basingstoke visitation 18th Sept., 1805. P. W. Hale and T. Snelling."

These entries continue several times and then cease.

1808. Constant mention of soldiers, Bedford Militia, Oxford Militia buried.

1814. Several soldiers of the 66th Regt. of Foot buried.

In 1811, Nov. 8th, a French prisoner (name unknown) aged 30, was buried ; and on 19th Dec., in 1812, a French prisoner, name unknown.

At the end of 1812 an entry is made, viz. :—

" At this period new Registers were entered on by Act of Parliament.
                    Henry Gauntlett, Curate of Alton."

And have continued so ever since.

Odd Entries. On a fly-leaf, at the end of the Parish Registers, are found the following odd entries :—

"Caleb and Joshua entered into God's Rest, none of the children of Israell entered in but they in the promised lande."

" The surplese washed the last weeke in Aug., 1669."

" The surplis washed the weeke before palme Sonday, 1666."

" The surplis only washed against Whitsuntide, 1666."

" 1666 Communion, Ester."

" pacient Sonday at Hart 1 pottle and 3 loaves of bred."

" Palme Sonday at Swan i pottle 3 loaves."

" Easter Day at Hart 1 P^{ot} 3 loaves bred."

" Sonday after Easter at Swan i galon i quart and 3 loaves bred."

" The second Sonday after Ester at Hart 5 quarts 3 loaves bred."

" Whit Sonday at Swan 5 pints 6 gals of Wine, 3 loaves."

" The next Sunday followinge at Hart 2 quarts, 3 loaves."

THE CHURCH AND PAROCHIAL CUSTOMS, AS OBTAINED FROM THE CHURCHWARDENS' AND VESTRY BOOKS.

The Churchwardens' Accounts date back in the old book as far as 1625, and they contain a valuable collection of records of considerable local interest.

There are entries of payment, or as often expressed, " Layed out," for ringing the knell, digging graves, salaries to sexton, clerk, tything man and constables, attending visitations, and the dinners on these occasions, cleaning the church plate, washing the surplices and church linen, Communion bread and wine, etc.

It appears to have been the custom to elect three churchwardens yearly. The annual meeting was generally held during the month of April and the Church rates made and collected at this time.

For each adult burial in the Church a charge was made for breaking the ground of 6 shillings and 8 pence, and for a child 3 shillings and 4 pence.

A shilling was paid for each seat allotted in the Church.

It seems to have been customary to pay an annual sum for the relief of maimed soldiers and prisoners to the Marshalsea, and sometimes the King's house (King's Bench).

The following are selections from some of the accounts of entries of exceptional character during various years, and there is sufficient evidence to shew the loyal spirit of the people of Alton by the various disbursements made by the churchwardens :—

April 1635 Layde out for Ringing when the Kinge (Charles I) came through ye Towne,   0   2   6

1639.   Ringing for Coronation day.

1669.   Paid for Ringing when the King (Charles II) came by,   0 15   0

1684.   To ye Ringers when his Matie rode to Winton   1   0   0

    „   „   „   „   ye Duke   „   „   0 16   0

    „   „   „   „   „   returned fr Winton 0 10   0

    „   „   „   upon his Matie return fr. Winton 0 13   0

1684, Oct.   Pay^d to Ringers when the King was reclaymed   1   0   0

Pay^d for a paper for the minister to enter ye Kinge
　　name in ye Common prayer Booke　　　　　 o　1　o
1685 P^d. to the Sexton when the King was crowned　o　1　o
1686 P^d. the Ringers when the Bishop came by　　　5　o
1702 To the Ringers on Proclaiming Queen Anne　　10　o
　　To the Ringers on the Queens Coronation Day　10　o.
　　To the Ringers on a Thanksgiving day for a vic-
　　　　tory at sea　　　　　　　　　　　　　10　o
1714 To the Ringers when King George was crowned 1　o　o

The Ringers were paid to ring on all such occasions as
the King's Coronation and Birthday, the Queen's and
Prince's Birthdays, the 29th of May and the 5th of
November.

Amongst the various entries of disbursements the following are frequent, namely :—

1694 "Given to Travellers and to several persons burnt out
by fire and other accidents and for lodging criples the sum of
£2. 1. 10."

"1714 Paid to disabled seamen and soldiers at times 15s. 1od.
　　Gave a man or a woman with a pass　　1 shilling
　　　,,　a soldiers wife and children　　 1　,,
　　　,,　a soldier with a pass　　　　　 1　,,

"Cleaning the Walks, winding the Clock, Repairing the windows, the Bells and timbers and new bell ropes, conveying the
engine to a fire, &c."

Under the head of "Penaltyes," an entry is occasionally
made fining a person 5s. for breaking of the Sabbath, and
3s. 4d. for being found in an alehouse on the Sabbath day.

"Rec^d. of Francis Smith, Constable, fower shillings wh. he
rcv^d. of Richard Merriett, Henry Searle, William Bunch, and
Edward Eyles by order of St. John Norton Bart one of his
Maties Justices of ye Peace of ye County afors^d. being py^d. a
piece by him sett on them for fishing in Cutpound River in Alton
whoe now presented for that offence by Thomas Chafin, Esq.
Lord of the Manno^r of Alton Westbrooke in ye s^d County."

"Recd. of one William Berry for being tipling in an Ale house
on the Sabbath day, one shilling."

Extracts under the heading—

"A Rate made for the Relief of the Poor of the Parish of Alton April 12th 1740."

Poor Rate. 1740.

"More for Cantsingers house and land		7	6
"Thoˢ Baker for Mill's Tanyard, house and Hatchers		6	0
"Thomas Baverstock for the George Inn		10	6
"Thomas Knight for the Swan Inn		16	6
"Mrs. Parker for the Parsonage	12	0	0
"John Gunner for the Five Bells		3	9
"Thoˢ Eyers for Wyards Farm	3	0	0
"Joseph White for Beach Farm	4	4	9
"John Gold for Thidden Farm	4	17	6
"John Gunner for Willhall Farm	6	0	0
"John Gregg for the Starr Alehouse		1	6
"Revᵈ Mʳ Bracebridge for late Dʳ Leech's house		4	6
"Ann Godfrey for the Crown Inn		7	6
"Dʳ Curtis for his house		4	6
"Wᵈ Wise for the Queen's head		1	6
"Matthew Gilbert for the Hart Inn		15	0
"Revᵈ Mr. Smith for the Vicarage '	3	0	0
"George Inwood for Tronchonts farm	3	0	0 "

Under the heading of "Disbursements for the Alton Poor," a few items may be mentioned to shew the kind of entries made.

Disbursements for Alton Poor. 1740.

1740. Expenses at Workhouse for 55 weeks	174	10	11
Pᵈ woman with a pass		1	0
Pᵈ Sailor being sick and pass		1	6
Pᵈ Old Soldier with pass			6
Pᵈ 5 Soldiers wives with passes		2	6
Pᵈ for an Ass to carry Jane Bramleys			
Daughter and her children to Norwitch		7	0

Gave her in money 1. 6. and pᵈ for two hampers for her 1 6

Pᵈ for an order to remove Mary Norris 2. 0. and for 3 horses to carry her off 6. 6.   Pᵈ Charles Parrack for going with her and their expenses 3. 0.

Pᵈ for playing the Engine 5. 0.
  Oyle for the Engine   1. 6.

1741 Pᵈ a Frenchman 6 passes and his expenses 1. 6.

1746 To Wᵐ Spurrier for cleaning the Church Engine and Oyling and Tallowing the leather pipe 2. 6.

1755 Pᵈ for two letters.   Mrs. Watson a bill for nursing yᵉ Smallpox &c."

In 1806 sparrows were paid for by the dozen, the last entry for sparrows' heads being in April, 1858.

Hedgehogs were also paid for.

Briefs 1666. A Brief was a Royal letter which was sent to the Bishops and by them to their Clergy, authorizing and desiring the collection of alms in Church during time of divine service for some specified object, such as restoring churches, fires and other charitable purposes.

Notice of Briefs being collected in Alton Church is first mentioned in 1666 and continue from time to time for some years. The Custom was given up by Government in the year 1853.

Extracts from Alton Parish Vestry Minute Book :—

" A fine Damask Cloath was given to y^e Communion Table of this Parish by an unknown Hand, being used y^e first time on Palm Sunday A.D. $172\frac{2}{3}$ on 10th Day. J. Sumner, Cur: first administered y^e Sacram^t."

" We Also Desire The Consent of this Vestry To Take Down The Glass From That Window behind The Pullpitt and Glass it again with Large Square Crown Glass In Order To Give a Better Light and also To Alter The Sounding Board In such a manner as shall be Thought Most Proper Upon the Opinion of The Rev. Mr. Smith Vicar and The Workman. Witness our Hands In Public Vestry In the Parish Church of Alton In the County of Southton This Twelfth Day of August 1742."

" We whose names are here unto subscribed at a Vestry held the 16th day of August 1756 at the parrish Church Alton do consent and agree that the Churchwardens shall lay out the money subscribed by several of the inhabitants for white washing the Church as Mr. Parker's Chancel is— but if it should so hapen that the money so subscribed should not be sufficient to do it we do consent the money wanting shall be paid out of the money which the Churchwardens now have in hand paid to them by the late Churchwardens as Witness our hands."

There appears to have been a manufacturing concern

of this Parish, but there is no evidence when it was started
or what the manufactory was, but it was given up in 1811.

1812. " Memorand on Fly leaf ' A Sermon to be
preached in the afternoon of Xmas Day wh. is attach^d *to
the evening Lecture* but not the necessary duty of the Incumbent.　　　　Churchwardens' Inf^n Xmas 1812."

" We whose names are hereunto subscribed Inhabitants
of the Parish of Alton in the County of Southampton met
and assembled at a Vestry this day, Tuesday, the 13th of
December 1814, held in the Parish Church of Alton aforesaid pursuant to a notice given for that purpose on Sundays
the 19th and 26th of November and the 4th and 11th of
December respectively, to consider of the propriety of
making some alterations in the body and other parts of the
Church, in so far as regards the seating of the Inhabitants
paying to the Church and Poor in proper and eligible pews,
and the erection of a new gallery for the more com-
modiously seating of the labouring poor."

" That the several following proposals be adopted by
this meeting—that inhabitants paying to the Church and
Poor be seated according to their present families ; that the
pulpit be removed ; that the font be removed ; the *first*
near the singing gallery and the *second* near the Communion ; that benches be substituted in the space the font
at present occupies ; that the blank space over the singing
gallery window be removed and the King's Arms be placed
in a more eligible situation ; that the calculated expense
do not exceed Two Hundred Pounds. That such Inhabitants asking of the Churchwardens seat room, and
seats being allotted them, that such Inhabitants pay their
own expense in fitting up and altering such seats."

　　　　　　　E. Poulter, Vicar.
　　　　　　　H. Gauntlett, Minister of Alton.
　　　　　　　Wm Osborn　　⎱
　　　　　　　Wm Edwards　⎰ Churchwardens.
　　　　　　　E. W. Gray　　⎰

" In pursuance of the wishes of the above Vestry the　Appropriation
Churchwardens gave the following notice to the Parish-　of Seats. 1815.

ioners on Sundays the 25th of December, 1814, and the 1st of January, 1815."

"Those Inhabitants paying Church and Poor Rates who wish to be seated with their families must apply to the Churchwardens on or before the 2nd of January, 1815. The following names made application accordingly and were seated in the pews numbered against their respective names, according to the plan on the next half sheet ; each name had seat room in the different pews for the number marked against each respectively":—

Pew No. 1.—Mr. John Willson—Taylor	...	...	4 seats
,, Henry Passmore—Glazier		...	3 ,,
,, John Clinker—Blacksmith		...	2 ,,
No. 2.— ,, John Butler—Victualler ...		...	3 ,,
,, Robert Smith—ditto	...	...	3 ,,
,, Thos. Harrow—Victualler		...	2 ,,
,, Rd. James—Laborer	...	...	3 ,,
No. 3.— ,, James Windibank—Farmer		...	6 ,,
,, Jeremiah Bond—Cadwainer[1]		...	3 ,,
No. 4.— ,, Edward Faithful—Baker ...		...	4 ,,
,, William Lewis—Brewer ...		...	2 ,,
,, James Walker—Postboy ...		...	2 ,,
No. 5.—Mrs. Terry	...	..	...	4 ,,
No. 6.— ,, Lee—Anstey House	...	..	
No. 7.— ,, Baker—Amery House	...	...	
No. 8.—James Baverstock, Esq.	...	...	8 ,,
No. 9.—Mr. Newnham—Surgeon	...	...	8 ,,
No. 10.— ,, Thos. Edwards—Ironmonger	..	4 ,,
,, Henry Turner—Tanner ...		...	2 ,,
,, Richard Hammond—Grocer	...	2 ,,
,, J. Ivy Cotter—Attorney ...		...	3 ,,
No. 11.— ,, John Dyer—Carpenter	...	...	7 ,,
,, John Allen—Tailor	...	...	5 ,,
No. 12.— ,, John Fielder—Baker	...	..	3 ,,
,, Bact. Wilkinson—Postmaster	...	2 ,,
,, Peter Marsh—Gardener	...	...	1 ,,
,, W. Row—Watchmaker	...	...	3 ,,

---

[1] "Cordwainers" or "Cordiners,"—Shoemakers. The word is from the French, "Cordounier," derived from Cordonan, a kind of leather brought from Cordonan.

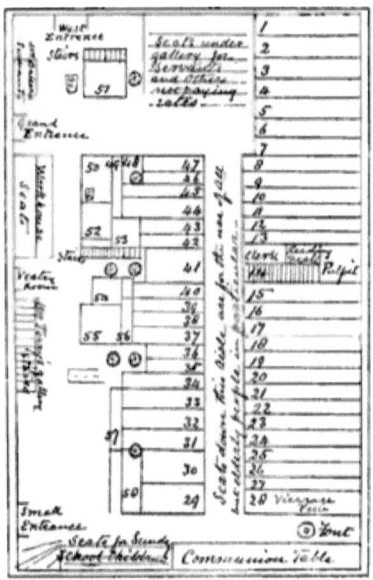

PLAN OF CHURCH SITTINGS,—1815.

Plate X.

No. 13.—Mrs. Glover ... ... 1 seat
  „ Edwards ... ... 1 „
  „ Greenfield... ... ... 1 „
  „ Bone ... ... 1 „
  „ Fielder ... ... 1 „
  Mr. R^e Davis ... ... 1 „
No. 14.—Pulpitt and Reading Desk.
No. 15.—Mr. Stephen Wickham, as occupier of Beech Farm.
No. 16.— „ Wm. Osborn—Collar Maker ... 6 seats
  „ John Dowling—Gentleman .. 1 „
No. 17.— „ John Chalcraft as occupier of Amery
  Farm and Lands.
No. 18.—Mrs. Ann Harrow, occupier of the Swan Inn.
No. 19.—Mr. John Camplin—Horsekeeper ... 4 seats
  „ Francis Allen—Taylor ... ... 4 „
No. 20.— „ John Baigent—Glazier ... ... 4 „
  Mrs. Bastin—Widow ... ... 1 „
  Mr. Wm. Barnfield—Printer ... ... 3 „
No. 21.— „ Kent—Grocer ... . 4 „
  „ Harding—Butcher ... ... 4 „
No. 22.— „ Yalden—Coachman ... ... 2 „
  „ Jordan—Auctioneer ... ... 2 „
  „ Baker—Carrier ... ... 4 „
No. 23.— „ Lazarus White—Victualler ... 4 „
  „ Charles Boswell—Butcher ... 2 „
  „ John Jeffrey—Cordwainer ... 3 „
No. 24.— „ Wm. Ford—Victualler ... ... 3 „
  „ Christopher Snowden—ditto . 4 „
  „ Richard Linney—ditto ... 2 „
  „ William Knight—Waggoner ... 2 „
  „ George Ralp—Baker ... ... 1 „
No. 25.— „ Stephen Isaacson—Gentleman ... 5 „
  „ Thos. Jeffrey Jefferis—Tanner 2 „
  Mrs. Pattern—Stamp Office ... 1 „
No. 26.—James Battin Coulthard, Esq.
No. 27.—Rev. A. Brett Docker and Sisters, by leave
  of the Rev. Edmund Poulter, Vicar ; this
  pew being divided from the Vicarage pew
  by a moveable partition which is taken
  out of the old chancel.
No. 28.—The Vicarage pew.

No. 29.—Mrs. Lamport ... ... 3 seats
       „ Godwin ... ... 3 „

This seat was claimed and allowed, as belonging to Mrs. Godwin by prescription, and immemorial use.

No. 30.—This pew belongs to the Executors of the late Charles Carpenter, as occupier and proprietor of Anstey Manor Estate.

No. 31.— Mr. Benjⁿ Bates Westlake—Schoolmaster 3 seats
     „ Wm. Dyer—Ironmonger ... ... 4 „
     „ Tho. Matthew—Glazier ... ... 3 „
No. 32.— „ Danl. Christmas—Butcher ... 8 „
No. 33.— „ James Tomlin—Brandy Merchant 3 „
     „ Wm. Hockley—Victualler ... 3 „
    Mrs. Mary Smith—Collar Maker ... 3 „
    Mr. Francis Heighes—Farmer ... 2 „
No. 34.—Messrs. James and George and David Ayling
       —Turners ... ... 8 „
No. 35.—Mr. Wm. Binstead—Ironmonger ... 3 „
     „ John Bunce—Farmer ... ... 1 „
No. 36.—Mrs. Kemp and Mrs. Willis ... ... 4 „
No. 37.—Mr. John Lock—Blacksmith ... ... 4 „
     „ John Gill—Baker ... ... 2 „
     „ Richard Watts—Broker ... ... 3 „
No. 38.— „ Wm. Edwards—Butcher ... .. 3 „
    Mrs. Scott—Victualler ... ... 3 „
    Mrs. Smith—Widow ... ... 3 „
No. 39.—Mr. Robt. Smith—Labourer ... ... 2 „
     „ Henry Gray—Farmer ... ... 2 „
     „ Robt. Inwood—Carpenter ... 2 „
     „ Wm. Woodman—Taylor .. ... 4 „
     „ J. Freyzard—Widower ... ... 1 „
No. 40.— „ Abram Biddle ... ... 4 „
    Mrs. Fielder ... ... 2 „
     „ Heath ... ... 2 „
     „ Grover ... ... 2 „
     „ Andrews ... ... 2 „
     „ Rothwell ... ... 2 „
     „ Howard ... ... 2 „
     „ Paton ... ... 2 „
     „ Lewis ... . 2 „

Mrs. Wheeler	1	seat
„ Isaac	2	„
„ Andrews	1	„
„ Knight	1	„

No. 41.—Vice-Admiral Sir Lawrence William
Halstead, K.C.B., Phœnix Lodge.

No. 42.—Mrs. Elizth. Dale—Schoolmistress ...	6	„
„ Mary Hellyer Cooper	3	„
No. 43.—Mr. Robt. Harrow—Baker	3	„
Mrs. Andrews—Widow	1	„
Mrs. Edwd. Andrews—Wheeler ...	3	„
Mr. William Barlow—Victualler ...	2	„
No. 44.— „ James Inwood—Carpenter ...	5	„
„ John Earle—Cordwainer ...	2	„
„ John Ventham—Labourer ...	4	„
„ John Lock, sen.—Blacksmith ...	2	„
No. 45.— „ John Trimming—Attorney ...	8	„
Mrs. Duncan, wife of the Rev. Jas. Duncan—Anstey	3	„

No. 46.—Mr. John Frost, 2 ; and Ann Oliver, 1.
No. 47.— „ Richard Blunden—Farmer ...

No. 48.— „ David Alderslade—Labourer ...	2	„
„ — Biddle—Cordwainer	3	„
No. 49.— „ Jas. Snelling—Watchmaker ...	8	„

No. 50.— „ Richard Marshall—Grocer ...
No. 51.—Thomas Clement, Esq.—This is a
faculty pew attached to some houses
in Cutpound.
No. 52.—Mr. Fredk. Gray—Merchant.
No. 53.—Mr. Samuel Smith—Brewer. This is a
large pew given to Mr. Smith to
accommodate a family of 14 children
who with himself and wife make 16
souls.

No. 54.— „ John Craft—Bricklayer	4	seats

No. 55.—Mrs. Trimmer and Family.
No. 56.—is the pew called the "Leg of Mutton,"
certain persons having claimed a right
to sit in it by virtue of giving a leg of
mutton, etc., to the persons occupying it before them.

No. 57.—is in the chancel claimed by Mrs. Terry in virtue of possession of the great tithes of Alton.

No. 58.—is similarly claimed. Capt. Green is the present occupant in virtue of his living in a house belonging to Mrs. Terry.

"The pews Nos. 50 and 52 were entirely built by Messrs. Marshall and Gray, by and with the consent of the present and former Churchwardens (see entry to that effect dated about 1804, some leaves back) and at their whole and sole expense on ground whereon never pew stood before, therefore Messrs. M. and G. have a *prescriptive right* to them *now* and *hereafter* according to the ecclesiastical law, which expressly says that pews may go from house to house by *prescription* and *immemorial usuage.*"

"*Two* pews on the *left hand* side of the landing on going into the singing gallery, *one* a *small* one, the *other large,* were erected in like manner by Messrs. John Andrews and E. W. Gray, and to which they have the like claim. This small addition to the singing gallery was made entirely by Messrs. Andrews and Gray at their private expense; of course the same observations apply to them as to Messrs. Marshall and Gray's undoubted claim. The three pews in the singing gallery are occupied by Mr. Thos. Jeffrey Jefferies and family, Mr. John Clark and family and Misses Edwards and Mesdames Bradley, Peacock and Binstead. The two pews on the left hand side on entering the singing gallery were erected by and at the sole expense of Messrs. John Andrews and Edward Wm. Gray by leave of the Churchwardens, therefore by prescription these pews belong to the parties occupying the same as private property. The front row of the great gallery is occupied by a pew belonging to Mr. Gunner as proprietor of the Willhall estate, and by a pew where aged men sit. The extreme back row is the seat adapted for apprentices and shopmen, and the row immediately before it is occupied by Mr. Saulez, Schoolmaster, for his pupils, with a part of another row, for which he agrees to pay an annual recompense of £3. 3s. a year to the Churchwardens for the time being."

"The gallery called the "Belfry" is occupied by the families of Mr. Thomas Levy, Mr. Henry Easton, Mrs. Mary Easton, Mr. John Cork, Misses Green and Mother, Mr. William Swain, Mr. Langrish, Mr. Andrews, Grocer, Miss Ronett and Mrs. Pearson. The 'Pigeonhole' gallery is private property (as see an entry to that effect in this book under date 1 Oct., 1796), and the parties claiming a right thereto sit there."

1831. "A Board of Health was appointed for the Town Nov. 15th."

1834. "At a vestry meeting held 1 Aug., 'it was resolved' that the boundaries of the parish be perambulated, and that the officers be instructed to take such steps as may be necessary to give this Resolution effect."

"A meeting to be held to consider the propriety of erecting pumps to supply water in case of fire."

"At a Vestry held 8 Aug., It was resolved, that a more eligible mode of obtaining water would be by erecting a falling hatch or penstock in the George Bridge, and that a Committee be formed to carry the resolution into effect."

1835. "The Parish of Alton was united with seventeen other parishes for the administration of the Laws for the relief of the Poor."

1840. "A Friend of the Church, this year presented to the Churchwardens, the munificent gift of a Crimson Velvet Communion Cloth, Cushions, Oak chairs, Carpet, Kneeling Hassocks, and Cushions for Communicants at the Altar."

1842. "At a Vestry meeting held 16 Sept."

"It was resolved that the Overseers do in obedience to the precept of Her Majesties Justices of the Peace return the names of the Thirty five following persons to act as Constables for the said Parish of Alton for the year ensuing." Then follow the names.

1850. A Vestry Meeting held 1 April 1850 It was resolved

"That the Cordial thanks of this meeting be tendered to the Vicar for so liberally responding to the wishes of the Parish in giving an additional service on Sunday evenings."

1857. "A Nuisance Removal Committee was appointed."

1860. "At the 25th March Vestry it was decided to tread the bounds of the Parish."

1866. "At the 1st March Vestry it was decided that as the boundaries of the Parish were well mapped out it was unnecessary to tread the bounds."

1867. "The Church Rates were discontinued and weekly offerings instituted this year."

1868. "At a Vestry held on April 13th, It was considered advisable at this Vestry to revive the office of sidesmen."

1869. "In Dec., The Vicar, the Rev. O. A. Hodgson, presented three Churchwardens' staffs of Office to the Church."

1870. "April. Miss Hutchins gave £100 for the restoration of the West Windows of the Parish Church. It cost £86 to restore one window. The balance was placed in a deposit Acct. towards restoring the other window at a future time."

1872. "At the 24th Feby. Vestry, The Parish were of opinion that as they were contributors to the County Rate, thereby having a paid body of men to discharge the duties of Constables, they were no longer needed."

ECCLESIASTICAL HISTORY.

1124.   "Alton Church was one of those which William Gyffard restored to the Blessed Peter, Prior Ingulf and his monks." [1]

"Bishop Godfrey granted to Hyde Abbey a pension of 40s. charged on Alton Rectory." [1]

1290.   "In 1290 the Rectory of the Church of Alton with its chapel was worth £60, a pension was charged upon it of 20s., and the Vicarage was worth £6. 13s. 4d. [1]

[1] Woodward and Wilks, p. 310.

"The deanery of Alton at this date included the
parishes of Aultone, Chautone, Faryndone, Estestede, Nywetone cum Haukele, Selebourne, Hertlegh, Froille, Bynteworth, Lasham, Shaldene, Worldham Major, Bientelegh (of which the church was not taxed), Colemer, &c."[1]

"The Deanery of Alton in 1535 included the rectories of Alton with its Vicarage held by Ralph Harriett, and worth £36. 7s. 8d. ; Colmer with Pryors Deane, Peter Bentle, £22. 17s. ; Bentworth, John Palmes, £18 ; Selborne with its Vicarage held by Milo Persoan, and worth £8. 2s. ; Lasham, Richard Scharp, £7. 4s. 11d. ; Estistede, Doctor Harpesfeld, £11. 19s. 9d. ; Faryngdon, Robert Fraunces, £19. 13s. 10d. ; Chawton, Thomas Wenne, £12. 16s. 8d. ; Shalden, William Pare, £10 ; Hertley Maudet, James Lockey, £10. 7s. 4d. ; Estwarleham with its Vicarage and the Chapel of Selborne, held by Nicholas Langrish, and worth £13. 8s. ; the Chapel of Chawton, held by Thomas Wenne, and worth 55s. ; the Chapel of St. George in Alton, and the Church of Westwarham, appropriated to the Winchester New College."[1]

"The Rectory of Alton was appropriated to Hide Abbey."

"In 1308, the Abbot of Hyde was fined 100 marks for leave to appropriate the Church of Aulton in his gift. The money was assigned to Robert Fitz Payne, seneschal of the household, towards his expenses in crossing the sea."[1]

Inquisitions of Ninths in the County of Southampton, Deanery of Aulton, Parish of Aulton.

"The names of the men of the said parish, Thomas de
Westcote, Simon de Heghes, John de Thuddene, Peter atte Mershe, Edmund Thurstan, John le Brut, John atte Devere, Nicholas Wiard, jurors, who say upon their oath that the ninths of the sheaves, fleeces and lambs of the said parish de Aulton are worth in the said 14th year £28. And they say that the ninths aforesaid in the year aforesaid did not amount to the tax of the said Church, because the

---

[1] Woodward and Wilks, p. 310.

H

said Church is dowered[endowed] with 1 messuage, 1 virgate of land, 2a. of meadow, pasture for 6 cows, 200 sheep, and 23 pigs, which are worth yearly 60s. and 23s. of rent. And they say that the tithes of hay, apples and mills with the small[minor] tithes, oblations and mortuaries of the said Church are worth per ann., £22. 7s. They say also that the ninths of the temporalities of the Abbot of Waverle in the said parish of which he gives tenths to the King are worth that year 50s., and that the ninth of the temporalities of the Prior of Seleborne in the said parish were worth in that year 13s. 4d., and that the ninths of the temporalities of the Abbot of Bells being to farm in the year aforesaid were worth in that year 20s., and that the ninth of the temporalities of the Abbot of Hide being to farm were worth that year 35s." [1]

"A Survey of the Rectorye of Alton with the Rights, Members and Appurtenances thereof lyinge and beinge in the Countye of Southt. parcell of the possessions late belonging to the Deane and Chapter of the Cathedrall Churche of the Holy Trinity at Winchester made and taken by us whose names are hereunto subscribed in the moneth of ffebruary *1649*." [2]

"By virtue of a Commission to us granted grounded upon an Act of the Commons of England assembled in Parliament, for the abolishing of Deanes, Deane and Chapters, Canons, Prebends and other officers and Title of and belonginge to any Cathedrall or Collegiate Church or Chappell within England and Wales, under the hands and seals of five or more of the Trustees in the said Act named and appointed."

"The Proffits of the said Rectorye Two Barnes and other necessarye outhowsinge conteyninge by estimc̄aon halfe an Acre, wee value worth fforty shillinges per Ann

xls.

"There belongeth to the said Rectorye the Tythes of all sorts of corne and haye within the parish of Alton, exceptinge the Villages of Kingsley and Bensted, which

---

[1] Lambeth Palace Library.　　　[2] Survey of Church Lands, *ibid.*

wee value worth one hundred and ninetye eight pounds. Communibus Annis   cxcviij.

"Allice Mason, widdow, by Indenture of Lease bearinge date 16 April 8 Carol granted by the Deane and Chapiter of Winton holds all the last menčoned premises withe the Appurtenances for and duringe the naturall Lives of Nicholas Mason, Edward Mason and Joane Mason, 3 of the children of the said Allice and the longest Liver of them, under the reserved yearly Rent of Twentye ffive pounds tenn shillinges, payable at the ffeasts of St John the Baptist, and the Nativitye of Our Lord by equall porčons, But is worth upon Improvement over and above the said Rent, One hundred, Seaventye ffower pounds, tenn shillings. Communibus Annis   clxxiiij^{ti}. x^s.

Redd' xxvti. xs.
Aporčoned
Lànds xs.
Tithes xxvti.
Will Webly
1641. May 8th.

"And if the said yearly Rent bee behinde ffortye dayes after either of the said ffeasts, then the Lease to bee void, and the said Deane &c. to reenter."

"The Lessee etc. to beare and pay all Charges and Taxes due and payable out of the said Rectorye during the terme afores^d."

"The Lessee etc. to keepe the premises and the Chauncell of the Parish Church of Alton in repaire at their own charge, duringe the termes afores^d. And if the reparačons afores^d bee not made within one yeare after lawful notice given to the Lessee, etc. The Lessee &c to forfeit to the Lessor, &c for every such default ffive pounds (nomina penæ)

The afores^d Allice Mason present Tennant Nicholas and Joane Mason two of the Lives in the Lease menčoned, both Livinge.

The Charge of repairinge the Chauncell of the said Church whiche the Lessee by Covenant is to Keepe in Repaire duringe the said terms afores^d., wee vallue at twenty six shillings eight pence. Communibus Annis."   ... } xxvj*s.* viij*d.*

"The Right of presentacon to the Viccaridge of Alton was formerlye in the Deane and Chapter of Winton being worthe ffortye pounds. Communibus Annis."

"The present Incumbent, Mr. John Carrill, put in by the Parliament.

Edward Hooker
James Quarles   } Surveyors."
Francis Hodges

ALL SAINTS' CHURCH.

All Saints Church.

Owing to the steady increase in the size of the Town, especially in the new district at the west end, the want of additional church accommodation was felt for some time. Steps were at last taken to erect a new church, and the foundation stone was laid by Sir Roundell Palmer, afterwards first Earl of Selborne, whilst Lord Chancellor, on the 18th of July, 1873. It was consecrated by Bishop Harold 1874. Browne on the 23rd December, 1874.

A parish was assigned to it, and the Ecclesiastical Commissioners endowed it with £200 per annum. The Church was dedicated to All Saints, and the sittings were declared to be "free and unappropriated for ever."

The architect was Mr. F. C. Dyer, of London, and the builders, Messrs. J. H. and E. Dyer, of Alton. The style is Early English, and it is built of Selborne stone with Bath stone facings. When erected it consisted of a Chancel, Nave and Transepts, and Organ chamber. It seats about 380. The cost was about £3,500. The stained glass windows in the Chancel were inserted in memory of Bishop Samuel Wilberforce, in whose episcopate the building was commenced. There are also three stained glass memorial windows in the south side of the Nave. The Organ, by Hill and Son, of London, was the gift of the late Miss Lydia Dyer; and the Font of Caen stone, bears the following inscription : "This Font was carved by J. Boggust, jun., and W. Pickett, in their leisure hours, as their contribution to this Church, 1874."

Plate XI.

ALL SAINTS CHURCH.—1896.

A Vestry was added in 1878, a Tower and spire, with three bells, in 1881, a clock, as a Memorial to Dr. L. Leslie, Treasurer of the Building Committee, in 1883 ; a larger Organ by Hill and Son in 1885 ; an oak Reredos and Pulpit, as Memorials to Mr. William Dyer, Secretary of the Building Committee in 1892, and a Chancel Screen in 1894.

During the incumbency of the Rev. Barrington G. Browne, a grant of £1500 was obtained from the Ecclesiastical Commissioners, and Queen Anne's Bounty towards the erection of a Vicarage, which was built by the Rev. F. J. Causton. The endowment of the living was, at the same time, increased to £300 a year.

The Sunday School and Parish Room were also added shortly after, the foundation stone being laid by Miss A. Augusta Crowley on May 18th, 1876. The cost, including the land, was about £900.

The building is used on week days as an Infant School. It is also used as the Headquarters of the Church Lads' Brigade, started by Mr. Reginald Crowley in 1895.

LIST OF VICARS.

Rev. Henry Castle Floud	...	1874
Rev. Barrington Gore Browne	...	1876
Rev. Francis Jervoise Causton	...	1877
Rev. George Covey Stenning	...	1886
Rev. Francis Henry Sumner	...	1892

THE ORDER OF ST. PAUL.
SEAMAN'S FRIENDLY SOCIETY.

The Society consists of an Order of Men, Priests and Laymen, separated and consecrated to the Service of God and our Sailors in Holy Religion. *Order of St. Paul.*

Founder and First Superior-General :—The Rev. Father Hopkins, O.S.P., late River Chaplain, Calcutta and Rangoon.

The Home work amongst Seamen is carried on at the Priory, Barry, Cardiff, and the work abroad at Bombay, Calcutta, Chittagong and Budge-Budge.

There is a Novitiate for the reception and training of workers in connection with the home organization.

1895.　Quite recently the Order has come to settle near the Town and is erecting some temporary buildings on a part of the Beech estate. Their settlement is known by the name of " Abbey Camp," and the building is to be used as a Home of Rest, as well as for training.

ALTON TOWN LANDS.[1]

1879.　The Alton Town Lands have for many years past been considered as vested in the Churchwardens and Overseers of the Poor of the Parish of Alton, who have been recognised by the Charity Commissioners, in sales and other dealings with the property, as the present legal Trustees thereof. The Trust embraces the four following properties, namely :—

" 1.—A piece of Garden Ground in Normandy Street, in the Town of Alton.

This was formerly the site of three cottages, which having become dilapidated were pulled down about the years 1850–55. The ground is No. 63 on the Alton Tithe Apportionment, and is therein stated to contain 16 perches. It is now let to Mr. Henry Woodman at an annual rent of £3, which has been received by the Churchwardens and applied in aid of the alms and money annually distributed by the Vicar and Churchwardens of Alton on St. Thomas's Day. This application of the income is not in accordance with the Trust, as the original donor of the property appears to have given " the rent for ever to place fatherless

---

[1] Report on the Charities of the Parish of Alton, by William Trimmer, Solicitor to the Alton Charity Trustees.

children, or those of poor estate, to some vocation whereby
they might live honestly, the officers to give an account of
that rent every year;" but the donor having omitted to
provide a repairing fund for the cottages they became
dilapidated and were pulled down as above mentioned.

2.—A piece of Land in Nether Street Fields in the
Town of Alton.

This Land is described in the Alton Tithe Apportionment as No. 483, and contains (excluding four perches
taken by the Mid-Hants Railway Company) 2 a. o r. 31 p.
It is let in small allotments to poor inhabitants of Alton,
selected by the Churchwardens and Overseers. The rents,
amounting to about £4. 7s. per annum, are received by
them and applied as part of the income of the Town Lands'
Trust.

There are no existing deeds relating to these two pieces
of Land.

3.—A sum of £624. 4s. 7d. £3 per cent. Consols.

This sum stands in the names of "the Official Trustees
of Charitable Funds," and has arisen from the Investment
of the proceeds of the sale of part of the above Alton
Town Lands, comprising Land in Normandy street, extending thence to the Line of the Mid-Hants Railway, and
sites of Cottages and Land in Amery Street and Lenton
Street.

The stock Receipts for the above sum of Consols are in
the custody of the Churchwardens and Overseers, and the
dividends are received by Messrs. Bulpett and Hall, and
placed to the Account of the Churchwardens' and Overseers' Parish Lands' Account.

4.—Mid-Hants Railway Rent Charge.

This is an Annual Rent Charge of £12. 16s. 6d., pay-
able half-yearly on 30th June and 31st December to the
Churchwardens and Overseers, by the Mid-Hants Railway
Company, secured by deed dated 24th March, 1873. This
Rent Charge was granted to the Churchwardens and Over-
seers as the consideration for part of the Alton Town

Lands taken for the purposes of the Railway, consisting of
o a. 2 r. 19 p., adjoining Paper Mill Lane, o a. o r. 11 p. part
of a slip of Land extending from Normandy Street to the
Line of the Mid-Hants Railway, and o a. o r. 4 p., part of
the above-mentioned Land in Nether Street Fields.

The above deed of the 24th March, 1873, is in the custody of Mr. Trimmer.

The income derived from this Trust has hitherto been
applied in aid of the rent of a Close of Land which is
rented by the Churchwardens and Overseers of the Perpetual Curacy of West Worldham, and let in small allotments to poor parishioners. The surplus has been allowed
to accumulate, and there is now at Messrs. Bulpett and
Hall's Bank to the credit of the Churchwardens and Overseers a sum exceeding £190, but this can hardly be deemed
a proper application of the income of the Trust."

GEALE'S ALMSHOUSES.

Geale's
Almshouses,
1653.

"This Charity comprises four cottages in eight tenements on the north east side of Church Street, Alton. It
appears that Thomas Geale, by his will dated 2nd May,
1653, gave to 'Eight poor people which should be born in
Alton, four tenements, with the use of a well and garden
plot thereto belonging, for their lives, to be chosen by his
executors during their lives, and afterwards by the Constables and three of the most honest and discreet men of
Alton, to be nominated by the Minister and Constables
aforesaid.' In the year 1824 these almshouses were occupied by poor persons of Alton Parish, placed there by the
visitor and guardians of the poor, but of late years the
occupants have been appointed by the Vicar of Alton."

STENT'S GIFT.

Stent's Gift.
1766.

"This Consists of an Annual Sum of £8. 6s. 8d.
granted by deed, dated 2nd April, 1765, out of a Messuage
and Lands containing by estimation 53 a. 2 r. at Wivelrod,
in the Parish of Bentworth to the Churchwardens of Alton.
This gift appears to have been made previously to the 45th

year of the reign of Queen Elizabeth by the will of John
Stent, unto the poor people of Alton, and the money was
thereby directed to be delivered into the hands of the Minister,
Churchwardens, and Constables of the Church and Town of
Alton, to be by them equally given and distributed to the
Poor people. It was originally a charge of £10 (diminished
by deduction of Land Tax to £8. 6s. 8d,) on Lands in the
parish of Alton. Mr. William Spencer is the present owner of
the Lands at Wivelrod, subject to this Charge, and annually
pays the above £8. 6s. 8d. to the Churchwardens prior to
St. Thomas's day. The money, with the annuities derived from Knight's Gift, Greaves' Gift, Geale's Gift, and
Goodyer's Gift, hereinafter mentioned, have been annually
distributed by the Vicar and Churchwardens of Alton on
St. Thomas's day amongst poor parishioners of Alton, but
by reference to the deed of 1765 it appears that the above
£8. 6s. 8d. ought to be distributed amongst the honest and
industrious Poor of the parish not receiving alms."

KNIGHT'S GIFT.

"Consists of an annual sum of £2 (reduced by de- Knight's Gift.
duction of Land Tax to £1. 16s.) payable out of Amery _{1617.}
Farm under the will of John Knight, Esq., of Chawton.
By his will, dated 15th August, 1617, this yearly rent is
given towards the relief of the Poor of the Parish of Alton,
with power for the Minister and Churchwardens to distrain
for the same. John Gathorne Wood, Esq., of Thedden
Grange, is the present owner of Amery Farm, and annually
pays the above £1. 16s. to the Churchwardens of Alton."

GREAVE'S GIFT.

"This also consists of an annual sum of £2 (reduced by Greave's Gift.
deduction of Land Tax to £1. 16s.), and is payable out _{1640.}
of lands in Alton, formerly Lamport's, now the property of
Messrs. Spicer, of King's Mill, Alton, under the will of
Sarah Greaves, dated 1st May, 1640, ' to the poor of Alton.'
This is paid by Messrs. Spicer to the Churchwardens of
Alton."

GEALE'S GIFT.

"Consists of a yearly rent charge of 40s. (reduced by deduction of Land Tax to 36s.), granted by deed dated 27th March, 1649, to Daniel Butler and six others, by Thomas Geale, to be issuing out of his meadow called Caker Mead, containing by estimation four acres near Caker Bridge, in the Parish of Alton, for 1000 years, to be paid over to the Vicar or Minister of Alton, and the Constables living in the same town, and to be by them at their discretion distributed amongst the Poor of the said Parish. The above rent charge was by deed dated 1st May, 1792, at the request of the Inhabitants of Alton assigned to William Lee and six others, of which seven persons, two were living in 1824.

"Edward Knight, Esq., of Chawton House, is the present owner of Caker Mead, and annually pays the above £1. 16s. to the Churchwardens of Alton.

MAGDALEN COLLEGE, OXFORD.

"This College pays an annual sum, varying in amount, out of the Great Tithes of East Worldham, in lieu of nine bushels of wheat, and this is annually distributed by the Vicar and Churchwardens of Alton. The College are the Trustees of this Charity, and in the year 1877 the amount received was £3. 3s., and in 1878 £2. 5s., which was paid by the Rev. Dr. Fell, Vicar of East Worldham."

GOODYER'S GIFT.

"Consists of a sum of £86. 13s. 4d., £3 per cent. Consols standing in the name of the Charity Commissioners for England and Wales. The gift arose under the will of Bartholomew Goodyer, dated 28th November 1789, whereby £50 was given for the use and benefit of the Poor of the Parish of Alton, to be by the Minister and Churchwardens and Overseers placed out at interest. The interest to be given away in bread at threepence a loaf the first Sunday in every month, to such poor old widows and widowers, old bachelors and old maids, as the Minister and Churchwardens should think most worthy to receive it, being inhabitants belonging to the said parish; but his will was that none should receive the bread but such as had been at Church prayers. The Stock formerly stood in the name of Richard Marshall, a Churchwarden, and was in the year 1873 transferred from his executors' names at the Bank of England into the names of the Charity Commissioners, who annually remit the dividends to the account of the Churchwardens and Overseers at Messrs. Bulpett and Hall's Bank."

MARSHALL'S GIFT.

"Richard Marshall of Alton, by an unexecuted Codicil (dated 1843) to his will directed a sum of £700, 3 per cent. Consolidated Bank Annuities to be transferred to the Incorporated National Society for promoting the education of the Poor in the principles of the Established Church throughout England and Wales, upon trust, to apply the dividends exclusively as a Permanent Endowment for and in furtherance of the purposes of the Sunday and Daily National Schools established in connection with the Established Church in the Parish of Alton. It appears that Mr. Marshall died before executing this Codicil, but his residuary Legatee, the late Miss Martha Hutchins, nevertheless carried out his intentions, and transferred to the Incorporated Society a sum of £700 Consols to answer the above gift." Marshall's Gift. 843.

EXALL'S GIFT.

"William Exall, of Amery House, Alton, died a few months before the above named Richard Marshall, and his widow, Mrs. Jane Exall, appears to have added to the above gift a sum of £200 Consols." Exall's Gift.

HAWKINS' GIFT.

"William James Hawkins, a son of James Hawkins of Alton, appears to have augmented the above gifts by adding a sum of £100 Consols thereto. Hawkins' Gift.

The entire amount therefore now standing in the names

of the above Incorporated National Society is £1000, £3 per cent. Consols and the dividends of the same are applicable to the purposes set out in the above mentioned unexecuted Codicil of Richard Marshall.

The deed of Trust relating to the above £1000 Consuls is in the custody of Mr. W. H. Moss, the Clerk of the Board of Guardians."

HUTCHINS' GIFT.

" The above named Martha Hutchins, by her will dated 19th January, 1871, gave a sum of £200 New £3 per cent. Bank Annuities to the above Incorporated National Society and directed the dividends to be applied exclusively as a permanent provision for and in augmentation of the usual salary of the principal Schoolmistress for the time being of the National Schools, in connection with the Established Church in the Parish of Alton ; and with the view of adding to the efficiency of such Schoolmistress ; but if at any time such National Schools should cease to exist in Alton, then the dividends of the said sums of £200 Bank Annuities should be applied by and for the general purposes of the said Incorporated National Society."

" The dividends on the above £1000, 3 per cent. Consols and £200 New £3 per cents., are received half-yearly by Messrs. Bulpett and Hall and paid to the account of the Alton National and Sunday Schools in accordance with the above trusts."

BAKER'S GIFT.

" It is stated on the printed boards in the Vestry of the Parish Church, that 'Mrs. Baker of Amery House left by will £100, the interest of which to be applied to the support of the Alton Sunday Schools.' The gift seems to have been made previously to the year 1820, but I have been unable to find the will referred to. The £100, however, appears to have been invested in Government Stock in the names of the Charity Commissioners, and the dividends, amounting to £2. 4s. 0d. each half year, are received by Messrs. Bulpett and Hall, and by them paid to the

Alton National and Sunday Schools' Account. The amount of Stock appears from the dividends to be £146. 13s. 4d. Reduced £3 per cents."

FISHER'S GIFT.

" This gift appears to have been lost to the Parish. John Fisher, of Bristol, by will dated 3rd June, 1741, directed his Executors to purchase sufficient land in or near Alton to yield £8 per annum, the trusts of which, 'as an annual allowance for three sermons to be preached in Alton Church, on the anniversary of his death, on Good Friday, and on St. Thomas's day, and for a distribution of bread and money to the Poor of Alton,' were contained in a separate letter of instructions, but unfortunately the direction to purchase land for charitable purposes was an illegal one. It appears from the Charity Commissioners' Report that Edward Fisher (the Testator's Nephew) who died in 1812 continued the Charity during his life, and set apart a fee farm rent, which he reserved on the sale of a small property near Alton. On the death of Mr. Edward Fisher in 1812, his Nephew, Mr. John Fisher, continued the Charity with the exception of the Sermon money which 'judging it might be applied more beneficially for the poor,' he discontinued on the death of Mr. Docker (previously to 1824), and until his death some thirty or forty years ago paid through his Agents as follows :—

Twenty Fourpenny loaves given by the Church-wardens of Alton on the first Sunday in every month after the Sacrament at the Church to as many poor widows who are appointed by the Churchwardens as vacancies occur and who receive the same during their lives if they continue to re-side in the Parish of Alton. } 4 0 0

Twenty Sixpenny loaves given by the Church-wardens at the Church to the same widows on St. Thomas's Day } 0 10 0

Twenty Shillings also given to them on St. Thomas's day— 1 0 0

(margin note: Fisher's Gift. 1741.)

On the death of Mr. John Fisher, his Brother, Mr. William Fisher, refused to continue the payment, except to those widows who were at that time recipients of the Charity, and no proceedings appear to have been taken by the Churchwardens to enforce it. The last of these widows, Mrs. Cassell, appears to have died in the old Amery Street Almshouses in 1876, and since that time no payment on account of this Charity has been made. A fee farm rent of £3 is still paid by Mr. W. J. Complin in respect of the Holybourne Brewery, and until the death of the late Mr. Henry Holding in 1873, this fee farm rent was received by him and paid over (less his payments on behalf of the Charity) to the Trustees of the late William Fisher. Since that time it has been paid to Messrs. Simmons and Clarke, of Bath, as Solicitors of the Trustees, and they appear to be the parties to whom any application with regard to the Trust ought to be made."

CHARITABLE DONATIONS

To the Poor of the Parish of Alton.

"1. Four tenements on the west side of Cut Pound Street.

2. One quarter of an acre, two and a half rods of meadow land behind the said tenements.

3. A piece of land in Lenton Lane, communicating with the said meadow.

1. 2. 3. The tenements, being dilapidated, were pulled down in 1877. The materials and sites with the lands Nos. 2 and 3 have been sold, and the proceeds now form part of the £624. 4s. 7d. Consols described in the Report.

4. Thomas Geale bequeathed by will dated 2 May, 1653, four tenements in Church Street with garden adjoining to be inhabited by eight poor people who shall be born in Alton.

4. These are still existing, and are described in the Report.

5. Three tenements in Normandy Street at the corner of Nether Street Lane, the rent to place, or help to place, fatherless or children of poor estate to some vocation whereby they may live honestly in time to come, provided always that they come of honest parents.

5. These were pulled down about twenty-five years ago. The sites are described in the Report of the Town Lands Trust.

6. Five tenements (since made eight) on the west of the upper part of Normandy Street, adjoining Chauntsingers field.

6. These were sold about 35 years ago. The purchase money was probably paid to the Guardians in aid of the Poor Rates, but it is not certain.

7. Two tenements (since burnt down) on the opposite side of the road, together with half an acre behind.

7. The sites of these and the half-acre behind were sold in 1873, and the proceeds now form part of the £624. 4s. 7d. Consols.

8. A shop in the Market Place, near the eastern corner of Cut Pound Street.

8. This appears to have been lost to the Parish prior to 1824.

9. Two acres of land in Nether Street Field.

9. This is described in the Report as part of the Town Lands' Trust.

10. Half an acre of land behind a barn called Spital Barn. An acre of land in Medstead lying in a field called Middle Field, and near a stile called Bar Stile.

10. This half-acre was sold in 1873, and the proceeds of the sale now form part of £624. 4s. 7d. Consols. The acre at Medstead appears to have been commuted in 1824 into a payment of 5s. a year payable by a Mr. Budd, but this has not been paid for many years.

11. A small piece of land at Redhill in the parish of Medstead.

11. This also appears to be lost to the Parish, until the year 1812 an annual rent of 1s. 6d. was paid as rent for this.

1. Mr. Benjamin Geale gave forty shillings per annum, payable out of Caker's Mead.

2. Mr. John Knight gave forty shillings per annum, payable out of Amery Farm.

3. Mr. Greaves gave forty shillings per annum, payable out of lands near Spital Mill.

4. Given to the poor out of Great Worldham Parsonage, nine bushels of wheat yearly always against St. Thomas's day.

5. Mr. Stent gave £8. 6s. 8d. per annum, now payable out of lands at Wivelrod, formerly out of property in the town of Alton.

6. Mr. Thomas Geale bequeathed in the year 1653 to the aged inhabitants of his Almshouses £4 per annum out of lands called Ravenhurst, in the Parish of Chobham, in the County of Surrey, but which lands cannot be ascertained.

7. Mr. Bartholomew Goodyear bequeathed to the poor of Alton £50, the interest of which to be given away in bread at three pence a loaf the first Sunday in every month for ever to such poor old widows and widowers, old bachelors and old maids as the then Minister and Churchwardens should think most worthy, but none to receive it but such as have been at the Church to prayers the day before they receive their bread.

1.
2.
3. These are still paid and and are fully described in the Report.
4.
5.

6. This appears to have been lost prior to the year 1824.

7. This is still in existence and is described in the Report.

8. Mrs. Baker, of Amery House, left by will £100, the interest of which to be applied to the support of the Alton Sunday School.

> 8. This has been invested, and is described in the Report.

1843. Richard Marshall, Esq., gave as an endowment for Alton Sunday and Daily National Schools the sum of £700

1844. William Exall, Esq., gave 200
James Hawkins, Esq., gave for clothing to poor and deserving children in schools every year 100
                                      ─────
                                      £1000

> These gifts are in existence, and are fully described in the Report.

Which sum stands invested in three per cent. Consols in the name of the Incorporated National Society for the Education of the Poor in the principles of the Established Church, the interest to be paid half-yearly to the Vicar of Alton for the use of the Schools."

THE CEMETERY.

This is situated to the north of the Town a short distance from the Church in Old Lane, or as it used to be called in former days Holy Lane. It comprises about 3 acres of land, a portion of which is unconsecrated. It was opened in the year 1856, the old churchyard being then closed.

Cemetery opened. 1895.

Churchyard closed. 1856.

The Burial Board was formed in the same year, 1856, and consists of 9 members, appointed by the ratepayers at the Easter Monday Vestry Meeting. Three members retire annually by rotation.

" In April, 1881, additional land was taken in for burials and consecrated by the Bishop," but even this addition has not been found sufficient, and the Board have recently agreed to purchase another plot of nearly 3 acres adjoining the Cemetery.

I

TOKENS.[1]

Tokens.

"During the troublous times of the 17th century the unsatisfactory state of the national coinage induced numbers of enterprising traders in different parts of the country to issue small copper tokens of their own. These usually bear the name of the issuer and the place of issue, and are of some little historic interest.

The main idea and reason for their issue were in many cases kept well in view, namely, that of being of essential service to the poorer residents. It will thus be seen that these traders' tokens have something to tell us of the condition of the country immediately after the great Civil War."

" 17th Century Tokens—Alton, Hampshire[2]:—

1. Obverse: OF . ALTON . IN, I.H. and T.B. In two lines.
   Reverse: HAMPSHIER, 1652 = W. W. T.
2. Obverse: Similar to above, but has I. H. and L. L.
3. Another similar to last, date, 1666.

1666.

4. Obverse : THOMAS . HARRISON = a griffin's head.
   Reverse: MERCER . IN ALTON = T. H.
5. Obverse: ANDREW . SARGENT = a pack horse.
   Reverse: MILLER . IN ALTON. = A.P.S.

Several Alton Tokens have been lent me for inspection by Mr. S. Shaw, of Alresford, and his brother, Mr. W. Shaw, of Brentwood.

1. Obverse: THOMAS BRA AN. T. B. in centre.
   Reverse: ALTON . IN . HAMSHIRE. H. B. in centre.
2. THOMAS BRAIMAN. T. B. in centre.
   Reverse: ALTON . IN HAMSHIRE. H. B. in centre.
3. Obverse: Similar to No. 1 above.
4. Reverse: Similar to No. 1 above, but has T.W.W.
5. Same as No. 2 above.
6. Same as No. 2 above."

From the Parish Registers I find that Thomas Braman was buried Feb. 10th, 1655. Thomas Braman, senior, buried Nov. 9th, 1661, and Thomas Harrison July 20th, 1674.

---

[1] *The Hampshire Antiquary and Naturalist,* Vol. I, p. 19.
[2] *Boyne's Tokens, 17th Century,* p. 97.

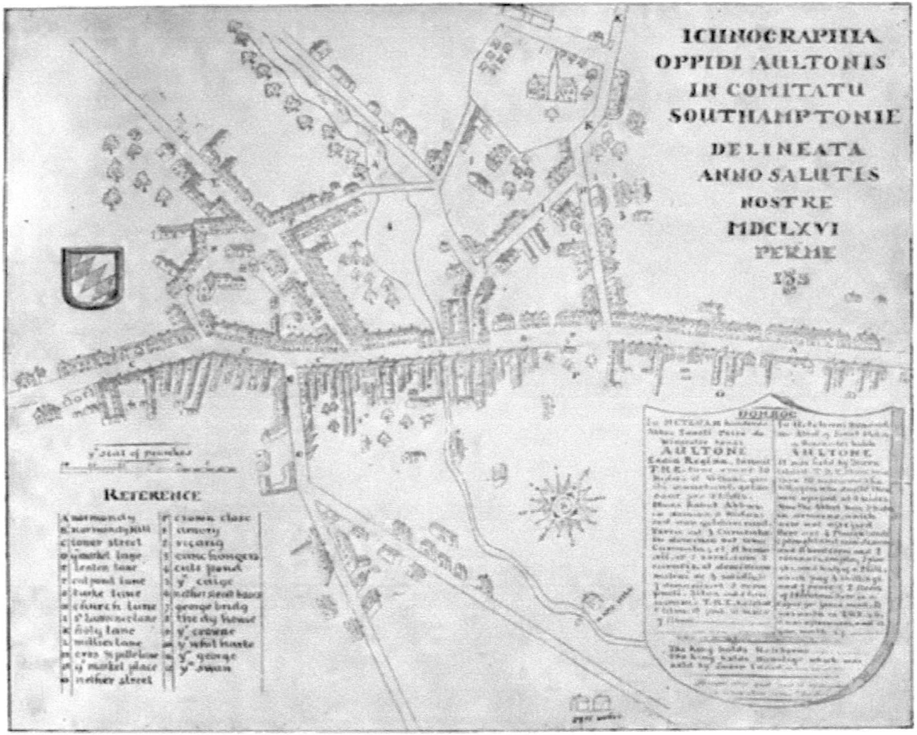
ICHNOGRAPHIA
OPPIDI AULTONIS
IN COMITATU
SOUTHAMPTONIE
DELINEATA
ANNO SALUTIS
NOSTRE
MDCLXVI
PERME
Reference
lower street
church lane
holy lane
nether street
vicarag
y^e crowne
y^e george
y^e swan
AULTONE

Plate XII.

Old Map of Alton.—1666.

THE OLD MAP OF ALTON, ETC.

The Old Map of Alton, hanging in the Curtis Museum (a fac-simile of the original in the possession of Montagu Knight, Esq., of Chawton House) is dated 1666, and it is curious to note some of the old names of the streets, etc. at that time. 1666. Old Map of Alton.

Church Street was called " Church Lane " as far as the Church gates, from thence to the Cemetery " Holy Lane." Vicarage Hill was called " St. Lawrence Lane " ; Tanhouse Lane, " Millses Lane." The further Market Street, at the side of Westbrook House, was known as " Cros and Pille Lane."[1]

Beside the river, behind the Swan and George Inns, was a house called " The Dy Howse " ; and a little further on " Hap's Mill," more recently known as Orp's Mill. This latter mill was used for cleaning and preparing flax ready for weaving. The Old Map also represents (what I can remember as a boy) that the old " Crown Inn " had a wide entrance archway in the middle of the house to the yard behind. The " White Harte " stood on the left of the Manor House and the " George " on the right. The " Swan " was in its present position but with a gabled roof much more picturesque than the present one. Some quaint extracts were fortunately copied from some panes of glass, now destroyed, which were found in a bedroom window of the Swan, namely :—

---

[1] " Pille Lane " possibly meant the lane leading to the Pillory, which stood at the end of the Town Hall.

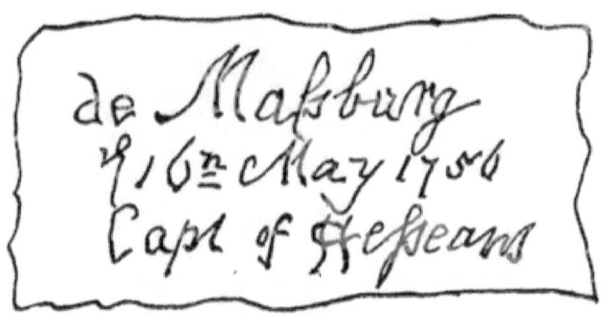

" Lieut Wm Bygrave of the
50 Regiment of Foot
God bless King Georg the 2^d
Fred Halsey 1718
Mrs. Devall
July 4 1791
for such a Cock as England never bred
Wings and Crowed without a Head
Halsey   T. H. Noyes Oct. 7 1755
1755
Down with   Alexr. Lawrence
the French   3 Septr. 1760
Bedford Balmerino."

About this time, 1666, the river crossed the street as an open stream, over which was a foot bridge, and two or three houses projected into the street. This stream was still open a hundred years ago, and was used as bridle road to Shalden through Flood meadow.

The manor of Chauntsingers was then spelt "Cauchongers." The cottages beyond Nether Street were called Nether Street Bares.

ALTON IN THE SEVENTEENTH CENTURY.

Alton in the
17th Century.
1784.
I am greatly indebted to the kindness of Mr. Johnson, of Winchester, for the inspection of a small Hampshire Directory, dated 1784, and compiled and printed by a Mr. J. Sadler, of Winchester. It is a very rare volume, and

Plate XIII.　　　　　OLD SWAN INN.—1845.　　　　FROM A PENCIL SKETCH.

I have copied all the information relating to Alton, which I believe will be found most interesting. It gives the names of the principle inhabitants and their various trades and callings, the inns, post days, coaches, waggons, etc. :—

" Alexander, Mrs., Ladies Boarding School.
Allen, William, Taylor.
Andrews, John, Carpenter.
Andrews, William, Wheelwright.
Baker, Palmer Richard, Clothier.
Baker, Mrs.,   Tanner.
Baverstock, Thomas, Surgeon and Man-Midwife.
Baverstock and Bowden, Brewers.
Bond, Matthias, George Inn.
Boyce, John, Brazier.
Bradley, Thomas, Draper.
Bristow, Richard, Fellmonger.
Child, John, Surveyor.
Clements, Mr., Attorney.
Clarke, Thomas, Staymaker.
Cooper,   Sadler.
Craft, William, Bricklayer.
Curtis, John, Tanner.
Curtis, James, Surgeon and Man-Midwife.
Dawes, William, Carpenter and Surveyor.
Easton, Mr., Post Master.
Edwards, Thomas, Ironmonger.
Fielder, Moses, Baker.
Gale,   Butcher.
Gauntlett, Thomas, Attorney.
Godwin, Thomas, Grocer.
Gold, Charles, Shopkeeper.
Greenfied, David, Shoemaker.
Grover, John, Collar Maker.
Harrow, Henry, the Swan Inn (Excise Office), and
        post chaise.
Harrow, Robert, Baker and Grocer.
Hawkins, John, Brewer.
Hewlitt, John, Baker.
Hoare, John, Collar Maker.

Holland, Richard, Barber.
Howe,   do.
Isaac, John, Gingerbread Baker.
Jay, James, Baker.
Jordan,   Cabinet Maker.
Johnson, James, Schoolmaster.
Kemp,   Surgeon and Man-Midwife.
King, William, Paper Maker.
Knight, John, Butcher.
Lee, William and Thomas, Mercers and Drapers.
Leach, James, Surgeon and Man-Midwife.
Long,   Attorney, and Distributor of the Stamps.
Love, John, Ironmonger.
Marshall, Richard, Grocer.
Martin, William, Barber.
Miller, Josiah, Shopkeeper.
Newlands, Daniel, Grocer.
Over, James, the Crown Inn (post chaise).
Page, John, Stay Maker.
Paice, John, Tanner.
Palmer, Richard, Clothier.
Palmer, George, Milliner.
Palmer, Edmund, Carpenter.
Pile, John, Taylor.
Roe, William, Bookseller.
Selfe, Jacob, Grocer.
Smith, John, Baker.
Smith, Henry, Sadler.
Snelling, James, Watch and Clock Maker.
Spiers, James, Glazier.
Temple, Henry, Hatter.
Tilbury, Stephen, Plumber and Glazier.
Walker, Mariner, Baker.
Waring, Samuel and Jeremiah, Mercers.
Waring, Samuel, Clothier.
Webb, William, Shoemaker.
Webb,   Jun., Surgeon and Man-Midwife.
Webb, William, Carpenter.
White, John, Basket Maker.

TANHOUSE LANE, FROM WATERCOLOUR SKETCH.—1844.

Plate XIV.

Post Days.

To London, Sunday, Tuesday and Thursday evenings at 6 o'clock; comes in from London, Sunday, Wednesday, and Friday, about 2 o'clock.

Coaches,

Collier's Southampton Coach stops at the Swan in going to London every morning, except Sunday, at about 10 o'clock; and on its return on the same day about noon; Inns at the Belle Savage, Ludgate Hill, London.

Clarke's old Gosport Coach, in going up, stops at the George every morning about 4 o'clock; and in returning, at the Swan, about 8 o'clock in the morning. Inns at the Golden Cross, Charing Cross, the Cross Keys and Spread Eagle, Gracechurch Street.

Another Gosport Coach, in going up, stops at the Crown about 4 in the morning; and in returning, about 8 every day. Inns at the Castle, Wood Street, London.

Gosport Light Coach, in going up, stops at the Crown, about 10 o'clock in the morning; and on returning, at half-past one every day. Inns at the Castle, Wood Street.

Poole Coach, in going up, stops at the Crown at half-past eight o'clock every morning; and on returning, every morning at 4. Inns at the Bell and Crown, Holborn Bridge, London.

Waggons.

Brookman's Winchester Waggons, one up and one down, call at the George on Monday and Wednesday evenings, and on Friday evening one down. Inns at the Rose, Holborn Bridge.

Clark's Gosport Waggon, in going up, stops on Tuesday evening at the George; in going down, lies there on Friday evenings. Inns at the Bell Savage, Ludgate Hill, London.

Fair.—September 29.

Market Day.—Saturday.

Mr. Long, Attorney, Distributor of the stamps.

Mr. John Boyce, Agent to the Royal Exchange Assurance Office.

A list of the Names and Places of abode of the Acting Magistrates, with the several divisions of this County.

Alton North Division :—

William Newman, Esq., Froyle.

Thomas Baker, Esq., Farnham.

Harry Harmood, Esq., New Alresford.

The Rev. Jonathan Dennis, Bramshott.

The Rev. William Sewell, Headley.

William Harris, Esq., New Alresford.

Alton South Division :—

William Joliffe, Esq., Petersfield.

Francis Hugonin, Esq., Nurstead, near Petersfield.

Thomas Samuel Joliffe, Esq., Trotton, Sussex.

William Battine, Esq., East Marden, Sussex.

Henry Bonham, Esq., Petersfield.

The Rev. James Cookson, Eastmeon.

The Rev. Joseph Bailey,   Sussex.

Dignitaries, etc., of the Church.

Rectories, Vicarages, etc., and their Incumbents.

Alton Deanery :—

Alton, Rev. Dr. Thomas Balguy, Vicar.

Binsted Chapel, do., do.

Holybourn Chapel, do., do.

Kingsley Chapel, do., do.

Bentworth, Edward Acton, Rector.

Bramshott, Jonathan Dennis, do.

Chawton, John Hinton, do.

Colemere, James Cookson, do.

Prior's Dean Chapel, do., do.

East Worldham, Dr. Richard Chaundler, Vicar.

East Tisted, Charles Prince, Rector.

Empshott, Richard Green, Vicar.

Farringdon, Herbert Randolph, Rector.

Froyle, Richard Pollen, Vicar.

Greatham, Richard Yalden, Rector.

Hartley Maudit, John Tuach, do.

Headley, William Sewell, do.

Lassam, James Pinnock, do.

VICARAGE HILL.

Plate XV.

Lyss, Richard Green, Min.
Newton Valence, Richard Yalden, Vicar.
Hawkley Chapel, do., do.
Selbourne, Andrew Etty, do.
Shaldean, Charles Page, Rector.
West Worldham,   Min."

COACHES.

" Till the beginning of the 18th Century we were almost wholly an equestrian people. Coaches began to be used somewhere about 1650. Pack horses and carriers' waggons for many years were the only conveyances for merchandise and passengers. Stage coaches appear to have been in use soon after the middle of the 17th century, but then progress was very slow. In the south of England we made more rapid strides towards perfection; and it was to its position on the great highway from Gosport to London, that Alton in former times owed much of its prosperity, for in the old coaching days the traffic was very considerable.[1] "

[margin note: Coaches. 1650.]

An interesting engraving of one of the coaches which used to run on this road, may be seen in the first volume of *The Land we Live in*. It was called the " Alton Machine," and in 1750 left our town at six o'clock every morning, reaching London the same night. This was then considered a marvellous feat. The Alton Machine was an immense clumsy vehicle, drawn by six horses, the coachman had four horses in hand, and a postillion rode a pair of leaders. The half-price passengers were not carried on the roof, but in a large basket, literally a basket, swung behind. The name "machine" became common, and hence stage coach horses were called " machiners."

[margin note: 1750.]

During the early part of this century a number of coaches passed through this town; three up and three down each day between London and Southampton, and London and Gosport. Two were called " The Age," two " The Times," and two " The Red Rover." There was also a private coach, driven by Mr. Yalden, to London one day

[1] *The Land we Live in.* Vol. I.

and back the next ; also two night coaches, one of which carried the mails.

Heavy road waggons for goods and merchandise, drawn by six or eight horses, travelled three or four times a week between London and Southampton.

Sixty or seventy years ago the mails were carried from Farnham to Alton by post horses ridden by post boys in blue jackets.

STOCKS AND TURNPIKE GATES.

Stocks.

Stocks and a Whipping Post formerly stood at the end of the old Town Hall, and also at Anstey, on a little piece of ground near the turning to Anstey mill.

Turnpike Gates.

A Turnpike gate stood near Dr. Stewart's house, but it was removed about 60 years ago to the vicinity of the Butts, in the position of the present drinking fountain. Another stood at the end of Lenton Street ; but it was removed about the year 1845 to Willhall Cottage, when the new Odiham road was completed ; and a toll bar stood at Wyard's end of Whitedown Lane.

MACADAMIZED ROADS.

Roads. 1819.

The high road from London to Gosport was made firm and good by a man named Macadam, who invented the process in the year 1819. The road-way was trenched to a certain depth, and all the large flints and gravel were broken small enough to run through a wire netting, or sieve, of a certain mesh. The ground was made good, and these broken stones placed on the top and well rammed.

Miss Jane Curtis informs me that she remembers the time when this was done thoughout the town, and that it proved a very formidable undertaking. She also remembers seeing Macadam, and knows that her father had frequent talks with him. This was the origin of "Macadamised Roads."

I have heard my father say that he was always given to understand that originally Normandy Hill was much deeper and more hollow than it is now, and that there was a bank covered with bushes, sloping down from the foot-path, and that Old Mr. Woodman, the builder, who lived in Nether Street, went bird nesting on this bank when a boy (between 1790 and 1800.)

MANUFACTURES.

" The old manufactures of Cloth and Silk survived in this County until the present century. About 100 years ago a brisk trade was carried on at Alton in plain and figured baragons (a genteel corded stuff), serges, white yarn, tabinets, bombazines, ribbed druggets and other woven fabrics, which found their principal market in America, and were much in demand in Philadelphia and its neighbourhood. At the same time shalloons (blankets) were made at Andover, and worsted yarn was spun in the villages round Alton. The silk manufacture was at the same time carried on profitably at Overton, Whitchurch, Andover, Alton and Odiham."[1]

" The Cloth made in Hampshire formed an article of commerce with the Venetians from the 12th to the 16th centuries, and was bought by them and shipped at Southampton. The festival of Bishop Blaise, the patron Saint of Clothworkers, has been celebrated at Alton within the last 100 years, and also at Andover." [2]

There was a Fulling Mill at Alton, called Orp's Mill, situated at the bottom of Crown Close, by the stream running into King's pond, and another at Millcourt, Froyle. This Mill in 1600 was bought by the Henry Wheeler of that time.[3] The cloth was brought from the loom, soaked in lye – fullers earth soaped—put into the fulling mill, and then worked dry until thick enough. Water was then turned on to scour the cloth ; the mill drew the serge or cloth in and out with huge timbers notched like teeth. When thus scoured the Cloth was dried in racks, strained out, and large fields were occupied in this way. When dry

[1] Shore' *History of Hampshire*, p. 270.
[2] *Hampshire Notes and Queries*, vol. vi, p. 144 (Shore).
[3] Woodward and Wilks' *History of Hampshire*.

all knots were picked out and the Cloth folded with paper between each fold ; after which it was put in screw presses, the first hot, the second cold.

Fuller's earth was found at Churt, and the mill no doubt served the Clothiers of Alton and Farnham. There was a great deal of local industry then and for a hundred years later.

Wool was spun at home and found a market close at hand.

Hop bagging was also manufactured here, and I can recollect seeing one or two looms at work in a room or store in Market Street.

Hollow turning was carried on, principally in the shape of wooden shaving boxes and bowls. There is a cellar window in a cottage (next to what is now Mr. Blake's foundry) which I found most attractive when a small boy, as I stood outside and watched the chips fly, while the old man, Ayling, worked at his turning.

There was also a "Walk" for manufacturing String at the back of the cottages on the top of Paper Mill Lane, and many a call we made on the old man, Palmer, to buy our string and whip-cord.

A little farther on, opposite Littlefield Road, stood an old shed outside a cottage, occupied by a man named Alwork, who made and repaired Cricket Bats.

At one time there was a Tanyard situated at the foot of Vicarage Hill, on the premises now occupied by Mr. Coleman and Messrs. Hetherington, one in Turk Street, on the site of Culverton House, and another was in existence during 1700, at the house in Lenton Street, now occupied by Mr. Burrell, and can only have been closed within the last thirty years.

FRENCH PRISONERS.

French
Prisoners. 1814.
During the Peninsular War, in 1814, the French prisoners often travelled through the Town and were sometimes quartered in an old building at the back of the Crown Inn. There was an opening or grated window

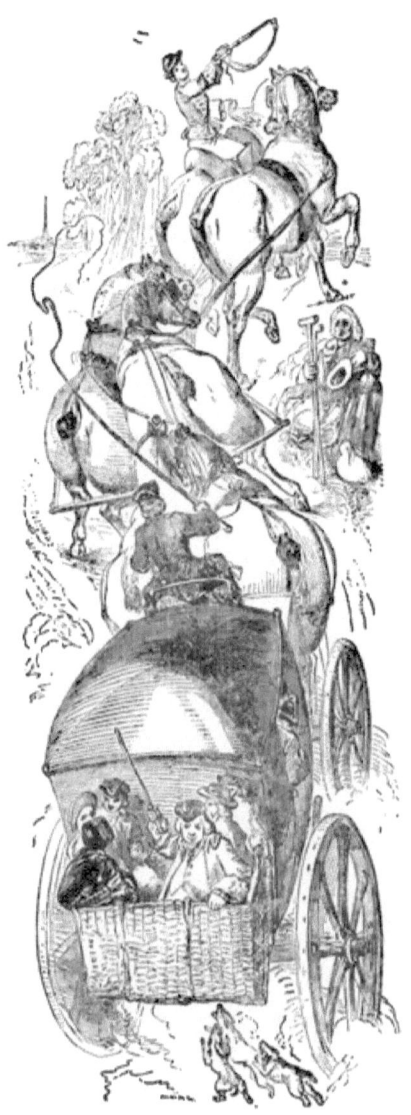

THE ALTON MACHINE.—1750.

Plate XVI.

looking into my Grandfather's garden, the remains of which are still to be seen, and through this my Father and some of his Sisters used to give the prisoners food and buy from them quaint carvings of bone. One of them made a hole through the wall and escaped by way of the garden to Great Wood, where he was captured.

In the following year, 1815, when peace was proclaimed, the event was celebrated by a public dinner in the High Street.

RIOTS.

"During the latter part of the Eighteenth Century the agricultural population of the County was in a distressed condition. Labour was abundant, work was scarce in winter, and wages low. The only County Schools were those known as Charity Schools. The bulk of the agricultural population of Hampshire remained practically untaught, and consequently when labour saving appliances, such as the thrashing and turnip cutting machines, etc., were first introduced, the labourers (who found employment in winter in threshing corn with the flail, as their forefathers had done from Saxon times downwards) were too ignorant to see anything in such an innovation except ruin for themselves and their families, and riots occurred in some places, in which the machines were smashed and other acts of lawlessness were committed." [1]

My father used to tell us of the excitement in the County on the introduction of machinery for agricultural purposes, and the general depression ending in Bread riots, about the year 1830. On one occasion he was riding on one of his rounds, through East Worldham, on his way to Kingsley, when he was met by a large crowd of excited rioters, who stopped him at the top of Worldham Hill, and said, " Oh, Mr. Curtis, it is a pity you were not at Headley when we broke into the Workhouse. You would have laughed if you had seen the tiles fly. Tell the people in Alton to look out as we are intending to attack the Workhouse and Breweries after we have been to Selbourne." My father on

Riots. 1800.

1830.

[1] Shore's *History of Hampshire*, p. 270.

his return home made known what he had seen and heard.
A messenger was sent on horseback to Winchester for
troops, and a number of the inhabitants were sworn in as
special constables ; the town was patrolled at night, and
every precaution taken against an attack   The guard
room was an old hop store used by the Messrs. Crowley,
and situated at the corner of Turk Street.   The pockets of
hops were ranged round in front of the fire place as seats
for the comfort of the night watch, and my father ended
his exciting reminiscences by saying, "Didn't I get a
welcome there, as the bearer of sausage rolls and home-
made ginger bread nuts."

Mr. Cassell, one of the oldest inhabitants of our town,
informed me that a troop of Life Guards came from Winchester, and were quartered at the Crown Inn.   They went
to Selbourne, when the rioters set fire to a public house,
and a barn at Newton Common, after which they became
disorganized, and did not attack the town.

It is quite evident that at the time of which we are
writing local information was not easily transmitted to any
considerable distance, and in consequence we find very
little information in the newspapers of that period with
regard to these events.   The only paragraph of interest is
the following in connection with Holybourne, dated November 29th, 1830 :—

1830.

"At Holybourne, near Alton, the labouring classes
assembled for the purpose of obtaining higher wages,
stating that the present allowance was really insufficient to
support their families.   The farmers met, and agreed to
give reasonable price for labour, with which the men
appeared perfectly satisfied, and returned to their work.
It is gratifying to observe that the conduct of the men
towards their employers was orderly and respectful.   They
declared they did not intend to join with any persons not
belonging to this parish, and only requested as much as
would enable them to live." [1]

---

[1] Extracted from *Hampshire Chronicle.*

The CROWN HOTEL
Commercial
FEARNISTER
Proprietor.
HALLS AND ALES.

Plate XVII.

HIGH STREET, ALTON—1896.

GENERAL DESCRIPTION OF THE TOWN.

The town is prettily situated in the Valley of the Wey, which river rises in the parish about half a mile west of the Town. Not far from its source it spreads out into a kind of swamp in which watercress beds have been formed. The stream then passes through the middle of the Town, dividing it into two parts, that on the right bank being called Alton Westbrook, that on the left, Alton Eastbrook. Just beyond the town it passes through King's Pond, a large sheet of water, originally constructed as a reservoir for the Paper Mill. Somewhat further on at Lynch Hill, it receives a small tributary, called the Caker Stream, which rises at Truncheaunts. In its course to Farnham, it is the motive power of several flour mills.

The Town is surrounded by chalk hills, and the neighbourhood is well wooded and picturesque. It stands on high ground, being about 250 feet above the sea level in its lowest part. It consists of one main street about a mile long, somewhat broad and slightly winding, running from north-east to south-west, and sloping from the two extremities to the river which crosses it near the middle.

As you enter the Town from the north-east, on the road from London, the suburb is called Anstey. The street is then known as Normandy Street to the top of the hill, which is called Normandy Hill, from the foot of which commences the High Street; this extends through the Town, the last part, towards Chawton, being known as the Butts road.

There are several side streets, the principal ones, branching off to the north, are Littlefield, Church Street and Market Street, continuing beyond the Market Square as Lenton Street, leading to Basingstoke and Odiham. Those on the south are the Station road, leading to the Railway Station, Paper Mills, etc.; Nether Street, Turk Street (in which are situated the Breweries), Hoppole lane, and Tower Street. There are several other smaller streets intersecting.

It contains a number of well-built and substantial houses with good gardens at the back. Most of the old dilapidated cottages have gradually disappeared, and the Town has, during the last few years, considerably increased, better-class houses, principally cottages, having been built to the north-east and south-west of the Town. Geale's Almshouses are situated in Church Street, and Normandy Cottage, for six tenants stands on the south-east side of Normandy Street, and was built by Miss M. Crowley in 1869.

On the south side of Normandy Hill is a Square, surrounded on three sides by public buildings, which form a very striking feature of the Town. The Cottage Hospital is on the south side, facing the High Street. The Curtis Museum and Art Schools, connected with the Mechanics' Institution, occupies the east side, and the Assembly Rooms the west. In the centre of the north side, contiguous to the street, stands a handsome drinking fountain. The centre of the Square is turf, surrounded by a roadway.

The Town is noted for being very clean and well kept. It is lighted with gas, and the footpaths are paved with bricks, and it is well supplied with remarkably good, pure water from water works situated on Windmill Hill. The shops are numerous and good.

The Town is in the heart of an Agricultural and Hop district.

The local industries are two Breweries, Paper Mills, two Iron Foundries, a large Building Firm, and a new industry lately started outside the Town for Photo Engraving work to illustrate magazines, etc.

The Hotels, Inns, and Licenced Houses are twenty-six in number.

The Town Hall and Corn Exchange stand in the Market Square. A Corn Market is held every Tuesday, and under the auspices of the North East Hants Agricultural Association, a Lamb and Stock Show is held on the Alton Butts in the month of July, and a Christmas Show of Fat Stock in the Market Square in December.

Plate XVIII.

THE PUBLIC BUILDINGS, ALTON. — 1896.

Two Statute Fairs are held during the year, on the last Saturday in April and the 29th of September, but, like most similar fairs, they have now nearly collapsed.

THE WORKHOUSE.

The oldest Parish, Churchwardens' and Overseers' Book dates from 1740, and continues to 1767.

A clause in the Will dated the 12th day of December, 1749, [and proved in Doctors Commons of] Thomas Harrison, Esq., is as follows, " Also I give and devise All that my Messuage or Tenement with the Malthouse thereunto adjoining and belonging together with the Courtyard and Backside and the Piece or Parcel of Land whereon a Hogsty is erected and built with their and every of their Appurtenances situate lying and being in Alton aforesaid commonly called and known by the Name of the Workhouse, unto the use of Anthony Baker, William Naish, Thomas Fry, John Dowden the younger, John Curtis and William White, Churchwardens and Overseers of the Town and Parish of Alton aforesaid and their Heirs, Successors, and Assigns for ever In Trust nevertheless for the lodging, keeping, maintaining and employing of the Poor of the said Town and Parish of Alton for Ever."

Workhouse. 1749.

" Alton Parish—Proceedings under the Act of Parliament of 22^d George 3^d, chap 83."

" For the better Relief and Employment of the Poor."

The following Notice was read in the Church immediately after divine service the 3 Sundays following in pursuance of the directions of the above Act, namely,

10th of June, 1792. *1792.*
17th „ „
24th „ „

Copy of the Notice which was read as above mentioned.

" Notice is hereby given that a public meeting to consult the owners or occupiers of Lands, Tenements or Hereditaments assessed after the Rate of Five pounds per annum, about hiring, purchasing and building a House or

K

Houses and providing for the Maintenance and Employment of the Poor of this Parish, pursuant to the Statute of
the Twenty-second year of George the third, will be held
at the Swan Inn, at Alton, on Wednesday, the 27th day of
this Instant June at 11 o'clock in the forenoon. Ben
Fielder, Clerk of the Parish of Alton."

"In consequence it was decided to purchase the Land
called Merriotts Purrock, on which the New Poor House is
to be erected, and certain persons be desired to act as assis-
tants to the Visitor and Guardian in framing and adjusting
the plan which may be thought most proper for the Poor
House intended to be built for the said Parish of Alton."

"The site and part of the grounds attached thereto
were conveyed by Thomas Knight, Esq., of Godmersham
Park, Kent, to William Webb of Alton, surgeon, and
Jeremiah Waring, of Alton, clothier, by conveyance dated
25th Sept., 1792, in which the property is described as
'a close of Arable Land called Merriott's Puttock, or Town
Close, containing about Three Acres, abutting on the West
on the King's Highway, and on the East on the River
called the Alton River.' The price paid was £110."

The Union Workhouse is a large red brick building
erected in 1792 at an outlay of £4000, and is situated at
the north-east end of the town.

The Rural District of the Alton Union, contains 21
Parishes; the acreage, 57,833; population, 1891, 10,475;
rateable value, £56,722.

THE GRAMMAR SCHOOL.

Grammar
School. 1641.
"This School was founded in the year 1641, by Mr.
John Eggar, of Moungomeries, in the parish of Crondall.
By an Act of Parliament, which was passed in the sixteenth
year of the reign of Charles I, entitled, 'An Act for John
Eggar's Free School within the parish of Alton, in the
County of Southampton,' it was provided that within this
parish a suitable school house should be built; that free-
holders of the hundred of Alton should be appointed as

Plate XIX.

EGGAR'S GRAMMAR SCHOOL,

TAKEN FROM AN OLD PRINT ABOUT 1820.

feoffees ; that these feoffees should have the power to purchase land, etc., for the maintenance of the School, and that they should nominate a schoolmaster. It is an interesting fact that the Act of Parliament referred to was the last public document signed by Charles I."

The School house was erected at Anstey, a tithing of Alton, and was unfinished when the founder died, which event took place on March 20th, 1641.

The endowment came from Mounter's Farm in the Parish of Chawton, and 37 acres of land at Anstey, etc. The Charity Commissioners, in their Report, published in 1825, state that there had been from time to time a surplus of income, and that such surplus had been invested in three per cent. consols. At the time referred to the amount thus invested was £550. The Master had a residence and about 2½ acres of land, and in addition to 24 Foundation Scholars, is permitted to take private pupils. The instruction prescribed is "Grammar learning" and Ancient and Modern Languages, Mathematics and a Commercial education to such Scholars as require it.

The farm at Chawton, and other lands, were sold, and the proceeds invested in Consols.

In 1879 a new scheme was formulated by the Charity Commissioners, and the School placed in charge of a Governing Body, under the name of " Eggar's Grammar School, Alton." A new School Room and Dormitories being added to the old building.

THE NATIONAL SCHOOLS.

The National Schools were originally located at the Town Hall, in the room now used as the Corn Exchange. At that time the market was held on Saturdays. When, however, the market day was changed to Tuesday, serious inconvenience was occasioned to the Schools, and fresh premises were therefore required.

National Schools.

The site of the School buildings and houses contains 1 r. 20 p., the ground being formerly occupied by the yard, barns, stables and other buildings belonging to the Rectory of Alton, and was by deed dated 25 January, 1841, granted by way of gift, by the Dean and Chapter of Winchester, the owners of the Rectorial Tithes of Alton, to the Rev. Edward James, Vicar of Alton, Richard Marshall, Esq., of Alton, and John Wood, Esq., of Thedden Grange, to be with all Buildings thereon erected or to be erected, for ever appropriated and used as and for a School for the education of children and adults, or children only of the labouring, manufacturing and other poorer classes in the Parish of Alton, and as a residence for the Schoolmaster and Schoolmistress; such School to be always conducted upon the principles of the Established Church, under the management and control of the Vicar of the Parish of Alton for the time being, assisted by a Committee of subscribers to the said School. The late John Wood, Esq., as the survivor of the above Trustees, in the year 1857 duly vested the Freehold of the above Schools (under the authority of the acts for affording facilities for the conveyance and endowments of sites for Schools) in the Vicar and Churchwardens of Alton and their successors. The deed of 25th January, 1841, is in the custody of the Vicar of Alton.

The buildings were erected in 1841, at a cost of £1396. A classroom was added in 1858, and there have been many additions since. The Schools are partly endowed, the following amounts having been bequeathed towards their support:—£700 by Mr. Richard Marshall, £200 by Mr. William Exall, and £100 by Mrs. Baker. In addition to these sums Mr. James Hawkins left £100 to augment the above gifts. The Schools are in connection with Government, and the first inspection was made by Mr. Mosely in 1845.

THE BRITISH SCHOOLS.

This School was started in Church Street, on November 20th, 1843; 29 boys and 6 girls were admitted on the opening day. On October 20th of the following year, the School was removed to a room in the rear of the Independent Chapel. As the number of scholars increased, the Committee decided to make this a school for boys exclusively, and according on January 1st, 1845, the girls were removed to Messrs. Crowley's Schoolroom in Turk Street. In 1849, the Boys School was brought under Government control. On the 1st of May, 1867, Mr. Frederick Crowley presented to a number of gentlemen acting as Trustees, a new British School, situated at the north-east end of the High Street. It is a handsome structure, built of red brick and white facings, and comprises a large schoolroom (capable of accommodating 150 children) and a class room. It was opened with a soirée and tea. The Girls School was removed from Turk Street to some new buildings erected in the rear of the Boys School in the year 1877.

The Managers of the Alton Elementary Schools (National and British), finding that their financial position was precarious and unsatisfactory, decided to take combined action to prevent the formation of a School Board.

In 1886, having enquired into the working of the Farnham Educational Scheme, which had been in operation for several years, with a voluntary rate, they recommended its adoption at Alton, and at a public meeting of ratepayers this recommendation was formally adopted.

It was agreed that each School should be under the control of its own managers, but that all moneys received, whether by Donation, Voluntary Rate, Government Grant, or otherwise, should be paid into a common fund. That a General Committee should be formed, consisting of Managers and Ratepayers, and that a Finance Committee should be elected from their number, by whom all receipts and expenditure should be controlled.

This Scheme has been in force up to the present date, 1896, and a Sixpenny rate has been sufficient for all practical purposes.

It having become necessary to provide increased accommodation, this was done by public subscription, at a cost of about £850.

The average number of children in attendance is, at the National Schools about 400, at the British Schools about 300.

THE FRIENDS.

" George Fox, who was born at Drayton, in Leicester-shire, A.D. 1624, was the first of the community commonly called 'Quakers.' Attired in his suit of leather, he started on his ministerial wanderings in 1647, and three years later his followers began to build meeting houses. There is no evidence as to the exact date when the Society at Alton was first formed, but this was certainly during the lifetime of the founder of the sect. The archives of the Society here extend, we believe, from about 1664."

1664.

" The present meeting house seems to have been used from 1672. The funds for the erection of the building and the purchase of the land were contributed by the Friends, and the list of subscribers is still extant. The old meeting house wall, next the road, has the date 1672 built in it. During the earlier part of their history the Quakers here shared in the general persecution of their sect ; a persecu-tion which emanated from a spirit of tyranny on the part of the Government, and of bigotry on the part of the English people. The following are examples :—

" The third day of the second month, 1664, Moses Neave, Clothworker ; Peter Bayly, Carpenter ; and William Wake, and Nicholas Gates, inhabitants of ye towne of Alton, were declared excommunicate, by Henry Butler, then priest or vicar of ye say^d towne."

" Nicholas Eade of Froyle was pronounced excommuni-cate in the steeple house (church) at Froyle by Richard Ffarrer, then Priest of ye said parish, and upon ye fouerth day of ye fifth month,, 1668." " Shortly afterwards Nicho-las Eade was persecuted by the Churchwardens of Froyle, and he was sent to prison for a considerable time."

" The 10th day of the 5th month 1670 wee were mett againe and as wee were waiting upon God, James May with two more called Justices came to us in ye house of

Moses Neave in Alton and pulled us out of ye meeting
and because friends would not depart at their command,
severall were abused, and they commanded Nicholas Gates
should be carried away, who was by 3 or 4 carried home,
and so they did for severall dayes so y^t in many months
wee had not a meetting within doors quietly but were kept
out in all weathers."

"Moses Neave for ye s^d Meetting had goods seized nigh
ye vallue of thirty pounds."

"John Inwood of Neatham had a horse taken from him
worth fower pounds, for his being at ye s^d Meetting and
for fouer more bodies besides himself wh. they fined and
charged it on him; his sonn paid ye fine without his
consent."

"Roger Gates for being twise at a Meetting and for his
Mother and Sister, once fined twenty shillings and had
taken from him in pewter and brass the value of fifty
shillings."

"We may remark that in the epistle received by the
friends in 1675 from the annual meeting of their body in
London, they were exhorted not to absent themselves from
their public worship in consequence of persecution, as that
would be inconsistent with the nobility of truth."

"In 1677 several Friends were cited to appear at Winchester 'for not paying to the repairing of the steeple house
at Alton; and soon after were pronounced excommunicate
by Henry Butler, Priest.' Three of them, including Joan
Sly, widow, were sent to Winchester gaol, where they
remained about two months."

"It is noticed that at the monthly meeting held at Alton
'ye 14th of ye 2^d month 1679,' it was decided to petition
the 'parliament men' respecting the sufferings of Friends,
and four persons were appointed to draw up a letter on the
subject."

The penalties inflicted on the Quakers at Alton tended
in no degree to diminish their numbers, for we find that
after the Meeting House had been built a few years, it was

too small to accommodate the congregation, and a subscription was raised in order to add two galleries. During the reigns of William III and George I, some acts of Parliament favourable to the Quakers were passed, and since that time the Society here has pursued the even tenour of its way without molestation.

THE CONGREGATIONALISTS.

The first meeting house of the Congregationalists at Alton appears to have been built somewhere during the seventeenth century by a person from Selborne, from which place Mr. Ferrol was ejected, and he first conducted the worship here. In 1696 the Chapel at Alton was opened for public worship. The first minister was a Mr. Foster, who was educated at Cambridge, where he took the degree of Bachelor of Arts. The congregation gradually fell off in numbers until about the year 1777, when there were only eight members. The Dissenters were at this period exceedingly unpopular. They could hardly walk down the High Street without being hooted at. Frequently the services were interrupted by riots at the door, or by parties bringing live sparrows into chapel in their pockets and letting them free during the service. Gradually, however, as people became more educated, a better feeling was evinced towards them.

1696.

In the year 1801 the Sunday School was commenced, and it was the first Sunday School in Alton.

The old chapel having become dilapidated, it was decided to build a new one, which was opened for divine worship on Tuesday, April 14th, 1835, the cost being £1035.

The Chapel was enlarged in 1868, and the organ, which up to that time had been used in the Parish Church, was purchased.

THE WESLEYANS.

The Rev. John Wesley was the father of Methodism, and the denomination was founded in the year 1738. The

first meetings were held in Alton towards the end of 1842 1842.
in an ordinary cottage. After a few weeks, however, a hop
kiln was hired, and the services were held in it for about
three years. This kiln belonged to the late Mr. Snelling,
and was situated in the rear of the premises now occupied
by Mr. Conduit. The Chapel was erected in 1846, and is
situated in the High Street; it cost £850. Recently it has
been entirely repewed and improved.

THE BAPTISTS.

The Baptists started as a small body in Alton about
the year 1840, under a Mr. John Forman, and in all proba- 1840.
bility held their meetings in an outbuilding, or kind of loft,
at the back of a house in Normandy Street, occupied by
Mr. Bartholomew, a Baker. After this, being very few in
numbers, they met at a private house. Some years later
they appealed for help to the late Mr. C. H. Spurgeon, and
by his aid they rented the large room of Mr. Cox, now
occupied by the Constitutional Club, and remained there
for about five years. After this they met with many ups
and downs, meeting in a private cottage for a time, then
occupying Mr. Cox's room again, and eventually, in 1891,
they succeeded in building a Chapel in Mount Pleasant
Road.

THE BRETHREN.

These started in Alton about the year 1882. They
first met in a private house, but since 1887 have rented a
large room in Turk Street, where they hold their meetings.

THE SALVATION ARMY.

These first began their meetings in Alton about the
year 1883, and opened their Barracks in an old building in 1883.
Cutpound in January, 1884. New Barracks were erected
in Amery Street in the year 1891, and were opened for
service in the month of September of that year.

THE TOWN HALL.

Town Hall.
1812.   The Town Hall was erected in 1812 on ground which
was afterwards found to belong to the Lord of the Manor,
to whom consequently an annual rent has to be paid.

This building is situated in the Market Place. In 1840
it was enlarged at an outlay of about £1000, and on subsequent occasions it has been altered and improved. The
lower room is used as the Corn Exchange and as a Drill
Hall for the Volunteers. The County Court and Petty
Sessions are held in the upper room, which is also used for
lectures and meetings. Further improvements were made
for the better accommodation of the Magistrates in the year
1893–4.

THE PHILANTHROPIC HALL.

This Hall, situated in French's Court, was built by the
late Mr. William Holmes, and is now in the hands of
Trustees. It will accommodate about sixty people. Its
use is granted at the charge of 1s. per evening for meetings
in connection with "sound philanthropic objects."

In this same Court is a house that was at one time fitted
up and used as a Workman's Club and Institute, which,
after four or five years, collapsed. It is now comfortably
furnished for the use of the members of the Young Women's
Christian Association.

THE ASSEMBLY ROOMS.

1880.   These form one side of the Square of "The Public
Buildings." The original scheme for these buildings was
formulated by Mr. Henry Hall, of the Manor House, and
the site was also generously given by him. A company
was formed to carry out the work.

The building contains a fine large hall with a raised
platform or stage at one end and small gallery opposite,
and capable of seating 500. In addition, there are two
good Committee Rooms (one being used by the Urban
District Council as their Board Room), retiring rooms,
cloak rooms, etc.

WILLIAM CURTIS,
Founder of Mechanics' Institution and Museum

Plate XX.

This building was opened in 1880, and in 1893 Mr. Hall enlarged and improved the stage and retiring rooms, and heated the Hall with hot water pipes at his own expense. The architectural design for the entire group of buildings was furnished by C. E. Barry, Esq., grandson of Sir Charles Barry, and the building of the same was substantially executed by the Messrs. J. H. and E. Dyer, of Alton.

THE MECHANICS INSTITUTION.

The Mechanics Institution began its career in September, 1837, under the name of the "Alton Mechanics' and Apprentices' Library." Mechanics Institution. 1837.

The late Dr. Thomas Hodgkin, was spending a few days at my grandfather's, when in the course of conversation, the subject of Mechanics Institutions was mentioned, and the desirability of forming one in Alton was discussed by my father, my uncle, Dr. John Wright Curtis, and others.

Very shortly after, a number of young men were gathered together, and a scheme was proposed, and adopted. This meeting included those who had signed a paper setting forth the objects of the Institution, and the means proposed for their accomplishment. It received 35 signatures, almost entirely of working men. The first organisation having been embodied in suitable rules, a working committee was formed, consisting entirely of quarterly subscribers. The business was for some time under the supervision, more particularly in reference to books, of a few of the supporters of the Institution. The Library opened with rather more than 100 volumes, some of which were presented, the remainder purchased by subscription.

The first local habitation of the Institution was in a store-room on the site of the house now occupied by Mr. Trimming's shop. The next or corner house of Turk Street was at that time a malt mill, worked by a horse going round and round with a great cogged wheel. At the back of this, extending up to the house now occupied by Mr. Moth, was a long malt house, and a dirty gutter, mostly overgrown with grass and other weeds, ran its whole length, forming a green edging to the street, rural enough, but not always in a sanitary condition suited to our modern sensibilities.

This room had a few years before been cleared out and fitted up for the purposes of Messrs. Levy and Baverstock's Bank, in a style which plainly shewed that in those simple times it was not considered necessary to spend money on appearances. The room becoming again vacant it was used by the Messrs. Crowley as a hop store, and whilst thus occupied it was lent for the purpose of a guard house during the riots of 1830.

Seven years after, the room was turned out and re-arranged for the accommodation of the Institution, in humble imitation of a lecture theatre, with two rows of seats forming three sides of a square, and raised one above the other, with a table in the middle. Here elementary lectures, chiefly given by Dr. J. W. Curtis, were kept up pretty regularly during two winters, their subject generally being Natural Sciences. In April, 1839, this place was given up, and the books removed to temporary quarters for about three months in a cottage in Church Street. Mr. Saulez' large school house, opposite Hoppole Lane, was then taken at a rental of £5 per annum, he having removed to Anstey Grammar School. The school room had been built by Mr. Baverstock for a ball room. It now makes one of the three houses into which that gentleman's residence was afterwards divided. Here there was better accommodation for Lectures, and in September, 1842, the 5th anniversary was celebrated by a dinner.

The next move was in August, 1844, to the Girl's British School Room, in Turk Street, opposite Mr. Pitt's shop, the event being celebrated by a supper. This room was the home of the Institution till its removal into Market Street in the spring of the year 1855.

The late Mr. John Bryant was appointed honorary Secretary at the end of the first year, *i.e.*, in November,

1838, an office which he held till the year 1869, when he
was succeeded by his son for four or five years, and Mr.
John Gale performed the duties of Librarian during the
greater part of the time the Institution was located in Turk
Street, and four years in Market Street. To the disinter-
ested kindness and persevering attention of these two
original members the Institution is very greatly indebted.

The Institution began with between thirty and forty
members, and for many years the numbers seldom reached
so high as sixty. It was not till the year 1850 that the
Lectures assumed a more regular and systematic character,
and that the growth of the Institution could be said to be
rapid. Up to that time Lectures (altogether gratuitous)
had been very uncertain, sometimes from six to ten in
number during the season, sometimes none at all, and
twenty persons made a moderate audience.

Dr. J. W. Curtis gave the first course of Lectures, and
many others during the next twenty years. He also
arranged a great portion of the first collection in the
Museum.

Dr. Stewart gave a number of very valuable Lectures,
and aided well in all the early uphill work required to
bring the Institution to a success. The late Mr. W. Terrell
Gunner also lectured, and gave very effective assistance in
a Natural History Class. The late Mr. John Cooper
preserved a large proportion of the animals and birds in the
Museum, and his name stands first of those who signed the
appeal to the working classes, calling upon them to found
an Institution for their own benefit.

1845 appears to be the first year that a report was
printed and laid before the public. It records slow progress—the Library consisted of about 600 volumes.

Lectures were better attended, and several microscopic
exhibitions were held during 1846, and the first balance
sheet is given—total income, £35. 12s. 10d.

In the year 1853 the Institution was received into
union with the Society of Arts, and in 1854 it joined the

Hants and Wilts Educational Society, and from this Society it obtained aid in Lectures, etc.

In the summer of 1854 "The Alton Exhibition of Works of Art and Industry, and of Natural Objects" was the greatest event which had marked the proceedings of the Institution. The Society of Arts sent about 120 photographs for exhibition, which became a nucleus, and the exhibition was for three weeks a great centre of attraction. Too much praise can scarcely be given to the ladies and gentlemen of the Town and neighbourhood for the promptness and liberality with which they came forward to second the efforts of the Exhibition Committee, by the loan of everything most beautiful, costly, or curious, which they possessed.

By the liberality of the public, the Committee were enabled to purchase the premises situated in Market Street. The Institution then well deserved the title of the "Mechanics," for the members carried out the work required to convert the house to its new purpose by working overtime.

The Reading Room and Library were occupied early in 1855; and the first floor of the Museum was opened to the public on New Year's Day, 1856, with a collection of about 4000 specimens. The upper floor was fitted up for a Local Museum in 1861, by means of a special subscription.

In 1858 a fourth soirée was held, and on this occasion a Service of Plate, consisting of a tea and coffee pot, sugar basin, and cream jug, and a handsome salver, were presented to my father, as Founder and President of the Institution, and bearing the following inscription:—

"This Salver and Tea and Coffee Service were presented April 8th, 1858, to WILLIAM CURTIS, by the members of the Alton Mechanics' Institution, as a Testimonial, for his liberal and persevering exertions in originating, and for his continual personal services in supporting it since its establishment, Sept., 1837."

This testimonial was purchased by a subscription, amounting to about 60 guineas, raised almost entirely by members of the Institution.

By 1874 the requirements of the Institution were largely expanding, and the number of members still increasing. The Reading Room and Library were not found large enough for the comfort of the members, and additional room was needed for amusements and recreation.

In February, 1877, a letter appeared in a local paper calling attention to the need of increased accommodation for the Institution, and also for many other public purposes, the old Town Hall not meeting all the requirements. This was followed by other letters to the same effect. About this time the late Miss Bell, of Borovere, wrote a letter to the Local Board, offering to present the Town with a drinking fountain if the Board would find a suitable site and supply the water. This proved for some time a difficulty, but eventually Mr. Hall generously offered a certain portion of Crown Close, with a plan to build thereon a Cottage Hospital, Mechanics' Institution and Museum and Public Baths, the drinking fountain to occupy the fourth side of a Square. Committee meetings were held, the matter fully discussed, and Mr. Hall's offer accepted by the Committees of each public Institution. The Public Baths were abandoned in favour of a new Assembly Room and Committee Rooms. The Cottage Hospital Authorities were enabled to build out of money left them for the purpose, and the Assembly Rooms were built by the formation of a company.

The Mechanics' Institution premises, consisting of the main building, the resident's cottage, drainage, furniture and fittings, etc., cost about £2360, which sum was principally raised by subscriptions and the sale of the old buildings in Market Street.

In the report for 1879, we find the following entry :—
" The Committee would call the attention of this Annual Meeting to the important step which the Institution is now taking—by far the most important since its first establishment—namely, that of the erection of a handsome building, well fitted to meet all its requirements. The Committee feel confident that the facilities which will henceforth be

afforded, will be productive of greater benefit to the Town and neighbourhood than the Institution has hitherto had it in its power to confer. The concurrent circumstance of the erection of a fine Assembly Room must also be a matter of congratulation, as it provides us with a commodious lecture hall."

The Report for 1880 says:—"The Committee have great pleasure in directing attention to the gift to the Museum during the past year of the large and valuable collection of Natural History, Geological and other specimens, which have been collected during many years by our esteemed President and exhibited by him, and which he has now formally presented to the Institution. It is owing almost entirely to Mr. Curtis' exertions that the Institution possesses a Museum, which for the variety and scientific nature of the objects exhibited, is scarcely equalled by any small provincial town."

" On Oct. 19th, 1880, the new Assembly room was opened and the Lecture season commenced with a dramatic and Musical Entertainment entitled ' The Chimney Corner,' by the Pickwick Histrionic Club. The Right Hon. G. Sclater-Booth, M. P., presided."

"On Oct. 21st, 1880, a Conversazione and Promenade Concert was held in the Assembly Rooms, the string band of the 82nd Regiment being in attendance. The Lord Chancellor (Earl Selborne) kindly presided, and in company with the President and Members of the Committee, inspected the various rooms of the Institution and Museum, and formally declared them open. They then returned to the Assembly Rooms, when the Lord Chancellor delivered an admirable address and presented an illuminated address to the President of the Institution, together with his portrait, to be placed permanently in the Museum."

In 1881:—"Almost immediately after the Annual Meeting the Institution experienced a great loss through the death of its late President, who had held that office for 44 years. Mr. William Curtis was the Founder of the

Institution, and by his devoted services for so many years, he brought it to a state of great excellence. To his knowledge of Natural History and long labour of love we owe our admirable Museum."

" The following Resolution was unanimously carried at a large meeting of the Members, held at the Assembly Rooms on Oct. 20th, 1881 :—

" The Members of this Institution desire to record upon their minutes the sense of the great loss they have sustained in the death of their late President, and their very high appreciation of his continuous labours in their behalf for the space of 44 years ; and they would specially note with gratitude that to the knowledge and persevering attention of Mr. Curtis, this Institution is indebted for its most excellent Museum."

At the same Meeting it was unanimously decided " That the Museum be known for the future as the ' Curtis Museum.' "

The year 1887 being the Jubilee year of the Institution, a Memorial Brass Tablet was placed in the Museum with the following inscription :—" The Alton Mechanics' Institution was founded in 1837 by William Curtis, Esquire, M.R.C.S., who was for forty-four years its President and the Donor of the Museum which now bears his name. In 1880 this Building was erected by public subscription, the Crowley Family being the largest contributors, on a site presented by Henry Hall, Esq., and was opened by Lord Chancellor Selborne on Oct. 27th, 1880. This Tablet is placed to commemorate the Jubilee Year of the Institution, and also of the reign of Queen Victoria, 1887."

Frederick Crowley, President.

Charles Stewart ⎫
Francis Whyley ⎬ Vice-Presidents.
John Herbert Dyer ⎭

In 1888 an Art Class was formed in connection with the Institution.

In 1891 it was considered necessary to enlarge the present building to meet the wants of the age in the

L

matter of Technical Education. Plans and estimates were obtained, but it was found to involve too great an expenditure to be carried out.

During the last three or four years various societies and classes have been started : the " Microscopical and Natural History Society," " Sight Singing," "Short Hand." " French," and " Commercial " Classes, an " Orchestral Society," "Dramatic Society," and " Cyclist Club."

During the year 1893 a very great and important step was taken in the purchase of Normandy House and Grounds, for the purposes of the Institution. The large and excellent pleasure gardens attached to the house have proved a great attraction to the members.

The cost was £1700.

The building was opened by the Earl of Selborne on the 3rd of October, 1893, in the presence of a numerous company assembled in a marquee erected on one of the lawns. In the evening the picturesque grounds were illuminated, and the Institute Orchestral Society's band was in attendance.

In 1894 it was found that since the opening of the Normandy Institution Extension the number of members had about doubled, and the issue of books from the Library had increased enormously. The total amounting to 26,174 vols., or an average of 503 vols. per week, against 342 vols. per week last year.

The old Institution building is now used for the Museum, and is also fitted up as Art and Technical Schools.

Fêtes are held in the grounds during the summer months, when the gardens are brilliantly illuminated, and the band of the Orchestral Society play selections of music.

QUEEN'S CORONATION.

1838.

Alton has evidently not been backward in its loyalty, for at the time of the Queen's Coronation, 28th June, 1838, " a subscription was started to give a substantial dinner to the poor of the Town. Tables were arranged on each side of the High Street, whole trees from the neighbouring woods were planted so as to shade the festive board, and branches of evergreens and bouquets of flowers adorned the doors and windows of the houses, a wreath of bays and evergreens spanned the High Street nearly at the centre, and close to it there was a triumphal arch with an appropriate motto. At six o'clock upwards of 2000 men, women, and children sat down to an excellent dinner. The toast to the Queen was given, followed by enthusiastic cheers, the band played the National Anthem, and a balloon ascended. Later in the evening there was a good display of fireworks, followed by a large fire balloon." [1]

The author has in his possession a printed list of the above subscribers to the above festivities, and an account of the disbursements.

PRINCE AND PRINCESS OF WALES' WEDDING.

"On March 14th, 1863, Alton celebrated the wedding 1863. of the Prince and Princess of Wales in a very loyal and national spirit. A magnificent triumphal arch of large and noble dimensions spanned the High Street, near the Market Street. The framework of timber was completely covered with trees and evergreens. On one side in large letters were the words, ' Albert and Alexandra,' on the other, ' England and Denmark.' The day was kept as a general holiday. All the infant school children assembled at the National Schools, then paraded the High Street, and were drawn up under the arch, when they sang an anthem composed by the Misses Crowley for the occasion, and set to the tune of the National Anthem. They then marched to the Town Hall and were regaled with oranges and plum cake. Later in the day all the children of the Town, about 1000, from five years and upwards, assembled at the Railway Station, and preceded by the band, marched in procession, carrying flags and banners through the Town. They were all drawn up under the arch, where they sang

[1] Extract from the *Hampshire Chronicle*, 2nd July, 1838.

the Anthem with the greatest spirit and enthusiasm. After this they were regaled with tea and cake at the Town Hall. The principal employers of labour provided a meal for their employées.

"In the evening there was a display of fireworks and a bonfire. The Town was also illuminated." [1]

RAILWAY TO ALTON.

Railway to Alton. 1852.

Alton was first connected by rail with London by an extension of the Farnham Branch of the London and South Western Railway, which was opened for traffic on Monday, 26th July, 1852. It was considered to be an event of such vast importance to the Town, that it was decided to celebrate it in a fitting manner. The following is a description of the event :—

"An enormous tent was constructed, 450 feet in length and 27 feet broad, in a somewhat semi-circular form, with a transept in the centre. This was covered with hop bagging and elaborately embellished with branches of trees, and ornamented with flags and other suitable emblems. The tent contained four tables abreast throughout the length of it, covered with white calico.

"Tickets were issued for 2330 of the resident working classes of Alton and their families. Tent room was also provided for about 100 of the same class from Holybourne. The inmates of the Union House also enjoyed a dinner in a tent on their own ground close by."

"The food provided for the dinner consisted of 3080 lbs. of butcher's meat and hams, in 243 joints ; 450 gallons of ale, 200 gallons of bread, 326 plum puddings, 168 lbs. of cheese, and a good supply of lettuces and onions. A considerable part of the meat was cooked at private houses."

"Upwards of 200 navvies were also regaled in a similar manner by the liberality of Mr. Brassey, the Contractor."

"A large pavilion was also erected for the Directors and Contractor and their friends to dine in, and upwards of

[1] Extract from the *Hampshire Chronicle.*

400 sat down to a splendid cold collation ; Mr. Edward Knight, of Chawton House, presiding."

"The first train, bringing the Directors and numerous distinguished guests, arrived a little before two o'clock. amidst the cheers of several thousand persons, the firing of cannon, and the playing of bands."

"After the dinner and the speeches that followed, dancing was entered into with spirit, and again in the evening by the thousands assembled."

"The festivities concluded with a brilliant display of fireworks, and the day will long be remembered in the annals of Alton."[1]

For some years after this line was opened, Alton continued to be the terminus, but later on a Company was formed to continue it to Winchester. This Alton and Winchester line was opened for traffic on Monday, 2nd October, 1865.

THE VOLUNTEERS.

In 1803, Alton must have had its own Volunteer Corps, 1803. like other towns, no doubt raised for the defence of the County, when an invasion by the first Napoleon was expected.

The following rules and regulations of this body have been lent me by the Messrs. J. H. and E. Dyer :—

Rules and Regulations of the Alton Loyal Volunteers.

1.—Every man not attending on the days and hours appointed for exercise before the calling of the roll is finished, to forfeit one shilling, unless he sends such an excuse in writing as shall be approved by the Corps, which written excuse will not be admitted if not sent one hour at least before parade time, to the sergeant of the division to which he belongs.

2.—Every man who (after the Corps has been clothed) shall come to parade not clean, or not properly dressed, or otherwise unfit for parade, to forfeit one shilling.

[1] Extracts from the *Hampshire and Southampton County Paper* and *County Herald.*

3.—Every one who shall talk in the ranks, or be wilfully careless, or inattentive to the words of command, to forfeit one shilling.

4.—Every man who shall quarrel with his comrades, or give them ill language, or give ill language to an officer or sergeant whilst on parade, will be expelled the Corps.

5.—All forfeits to be determined by the Committee for the time being.

6.—That there shall always be a Standing Committee to whom all matters of dispute respecting forfeits shall be referred, and that the said Committee shall consist of the commissioned officers and six of the Corps chosen by themselves whose names shall be entered in the orderly book.

7.—That if any man shall quit the ranks without leave he shall forfeit sixpence.

8.—Relates to the appointment of the non-commissioned officers.

9.—Resolved that the commissioned officers, and also Thomas Gunner, John Pattern, Bridger Bradley, Thomas Edwards, John Chalcraft, and Nicholas Allen, be a Committee for regulating such of the matters of this Association as are to be regulated by a Committee.

The Alton Volunteer Rifle Corps

Volunteer Rifle Corps. 1860. Was started in the year 1860, and gazetted on August 20th as the 21st Hants R. V. The uniform was a dusty grey with green facings and black braid trimming. In 1870 the Company was joined to the 1st Battalion. In 1877 the uniform was changed to scarlet with black facings and white Austrian knots on the sleeves, the head dress being the Glengarry (now changed for the new field service cap). In 1879 the facings were changed to white, helmets also being worn ; the uniform being the same as the County Regiments, only with silver instead of gold stripes.

The strength of the Company is now (1895) 84, including the band. Six of the members were presented with the " Long Service Medal," by H.R.H. the Duke of Connaught at Aldershot during the summer of 1895.

VOLUNTEER FIRE BRIGADE.

The Volunteer Fire Brigade was formed on June 15th, 1863. A brigade had been in existence in the Town for many years previously, but the plant was antiquated and the general character of the Brigade so unreliable in the case of a great fire, that it was the unanimous wish of the Local Board and the townspeople generally that there should be a reorganisation. Volunteer Fire Brigade, 1863.

The necessary funds were collected for the purchase of plant, the Brigade was started, and Mr. Alfred Hetherington was elected Chief Officer. A Paxton Manual Engine was obtained, but it was found insufficient, and a steam fire engine was purchased of Messrs. Merryweather in 1864. The " Firefly " was the first fire engine to leave the Metropolis for a provincial town.

In 1876 Mr. Hetherington resigned his post and Mr. J. H. Dyer was elected Chief Officer in his stead.

Alton people have been justly proud of their Brigade from its very commencement, and now, after over thirty years, the Brigade was never better organized and manned, while the plant is far more extensive and effective. Quite recently one of the most commodious and thoroughly equipped fire stations in the south of England has been obtained, situated in Cutpound, close to the river.

The plant includes a new steamer, " Firefly the 2nd," recently purchased from Messrs. Merryweather to replace the first Firefly, a manual engine in excellent order, a hand hose truck for the Town, and a four-wheel van for the country (which is also used to convey some of the Brigade and plant), a telescopic fire escape ladder, jumping sheet, life saving line and other appliances, and about 1800 feet of hose.

The Town is well supplied with water, and from the mains and numerous hydrants the Brigade are able to get quickly to work in case a fire occurs in the Town.

THE PAPER MILLS.

Paper Mills.   These are situated near the Railway Station, and stand
on the river Wey.   At the back of the mill is a large pond
called King's pond, through which the river flows.   The
mill originally belonged to a Mr. King, and a good deal of
the paper made here still bears the water mark, "W. King."
All the paper is hand made.

Mr. John E. Spicer took possession of the Alton Paper
Mills in August, 1796.   They were probably worked before
1700.

THE POLICE STATION.

Police.   In the old Map of Alton, dated 1666, the "Caige"
stood on Normandy Hill, on the site now occupied by the
Board Room of the Urban District Council.   This Caige
was still in use when I was a boy ; it was a sort of shed or
room with an old door, a window, without glass, only iron
bars across and a wooden shutter.   This was used as the
Lock-up.   The Hants County Constabulary was formed at
the beginning of 1840, but it was not till the act of 1856
was passed that their appointment was rendered com-
pulsory.

I find that "At a Vestry held the 24 Feb., 1872, the
Parish were of opinion that as they were contributors to
the County Rate, thereby having a paid body of men to
discharge the duties of Constables, they were no longer
needed."

The Police Station was originally situated at the foot
of Normandy Hill, in the house now occupied by Mr.
Ackland.   It was afterwards removed to the house next
the Red Lion.   The present Station was built in 1845 at a
cost of £1400, at the south-western extremity of the Town.
It has been enlarged and improved since then.   It is the
Headquarters for the Alton Division of Police, which consists of an Inspector, two sergeants and twelve constables.
It is occupied by the Inspector, one sergeant and a constable.   There are three cells for the accommodation of
prisoners.

GAS WORKS.

These are situated near the Police Station, on the north Gas Works 1844.
side of the Butts road, and were constructed in 1844. The
Alton Gas and Coke Company was constituted under the
Joint Stock Companies Act, on the sixth day of July,
1847, with a capital of £2500 in 250 shares of £10 each.

THE POST OFFICE.

About fifty or sixty years ago this was situated in a Post Office.
small house in Church Street, and the old lady who looked
after it delivered the letters, and in wet weather tramped
about in her pattens. It was next situated in a house on
the south side of Normandy Hill ; then it had several
locations in the High Street, and for some years was
established at the house now occupied by Mr. Cæsar.
With the increase of business the premises became too
small and the office was removed to larger premises at the
corner of Turk Street, in the year 1875.

Owing to the establishment of the Parcel Post and the
rapid increase of business, these premises became totally
inadequate, and at the death of the late Postmaster, Mr. J.
Bryant, the office was again on the appointment of his
successor, Mr. J. F. Parsons, removed to the present much
larger and better adapted premises in the year 1890.

It may be of interest to give a few details of the
business transacted in the office during the twelve months
of 1895 :—

Letters delivered during the twelve months	950,000
Letters posted ...	702,000
Telegrams forwarded and received ...	20,095
Money Orders issued	1,687
Money Orders paid	1,547
Savings Bank transactions	3,380
Postal Orders issued	24,010
Postal Orders paid	22,295
Parcels posted ...	22,000
Parcels delivered	31,140
Postage Stamps sold	£3,872
Inland Revenue Licences issued	£490

MESSRS. J. H. AND E. DYER'S WORKS.

Builders. 1784.   The Building Business of Messrs. J. H. and E. Dyer, in the High Street, is one of the oldest industries in the Town, having been carried on by members of the Dyer family since 1784.

During the past 110 years the firm has carried out many important works in the County, such as building and restoring churches, erecting mansions, public and other buildings, etc. The present members are sons of William Dyer and grandsons of John Dyer, the Founder of the Firm.

THE VICTORIA FOUNDRY

Foundries. 1846.   Was established by the late Mr. William Henry Blake in 1846, and carried on since by members of the same family as an Agricultural and Engineering Works.

THE WEY IRON WORKS

Are situated in Cut Pound, on the site formerly occu- pied by a brewery in the occupation of Mr. Fielder. They 1865. were started in the year 1865 by Messrs. Hetherington. The firm after a time changed to Hetherington and Moore, then to Hetherington and Parker. It is now known by the name of Hetherington and Co. The business works are principally for agricultural purposes, hop-drying appar- atus, and cart and waggon building, etc.

BREWERIES.

Breweries 1821.   There are two Breweries in the Town—one of very large size, which was bought by the " Messrs. Crowley of the Assignees and Mortgagees of the late Mr. J. H. Baverstock on 28th August, 1821."

This Mr. Baverstock was a literary and scientific man. He was born at Alton on June 10th, 1741, and when about 22 years of age became a partner with his father, and shortly after built the brewery in Turk Street. About the year 1768 Mr. James Baverstock purchased a hydrometer, and after numerous experiments made in this brewery, found that he could ascertain the comparative strength of worts by its use. This was a valuable discovery, and laid the foundation of saccharometry, now practised in all breweries.

The brewery was sold to the present proprietors (Messrs. Crowley and Co.) on 24th March, 1877.

The second brewery belongs to the Messrs. Hall, and is 1841. also situated in Turk Street. This brewery with the houses attached to it was purchased by Mr. Henry Hall, of Ely in Cambridgeshire, of Mr. John Hawkins, who was then living at Cosford, in Surrey, in the year 1841. Mr. Hawkins' manager was James Newman Frost, who was related to Cardinal Newman, and whose family were said to have been brewers at Alton.

WESTBROOK HOUSE ASYLUM

Is a private Institution, and was established by the Asylum. 1833. late Dr. Burnett, in the year 1833.

THE COTTAGE HOSPITAL

This was established in the year 1868 in a small house Cottage Hospital. 1868 at the west end of the High Street, well adapted for the purpose, chiefly through the exertions and kind munificence of the late Rev. C. Causton, Rector of Lasham.

In 1871 a legacy of £150, free of duty, was bequeathed by the late John Gray Duncan, Esq., of Alton.

In 1876 a legacy of £500 was left under the will of the late Henry Joyce Mulcock, Esq., of Ropley.

During the year 1877 a bequest of £1500 was received under the will of the late Mr. Daniel Inwood, of Binsted.

Mr. Hall, of the Manor House, intimated his willingness to present a site in Crown Close for a new Hospital, and his munificent offer was thankfully accepted.

The new Hospital was completed in 1880, and the patients were transferred on 6th October. On the following day a Dedication Service was held by the Lord Bishop of the Diocese.

The new Building, designed by C. E. Barry, Esq., of London, cost, inclusive of new furniture, etc., £2231. 2s. 8d.

The Hospital contains two large wards of three beds each, male and female, an Accident Ward and a Convalescent Room, etc. On an emergency eight inmates can be admitted, the usual number of in-patients being six.

NURSING SOCIETIES.

There are two in the Town. The District Nurse was established in 1882, her duties being to visit all cottage homes in cases of illness, free of charge.

The Maternity Nurse is worked as a branch of the Hants Rural Nursing Association, and was started in 1891.

THE ALTON URBAN DISTRICT COUNCIL.

Urban District Council. 1860.

The Alton Urban District Council, formerly the Alton Local Board. The Local Government Act was adopted here on 1st August, 1860.

The Council consists of twelve Councillors, elected by the ratepayers, four of whom vacate office annually by rotation. The Chairman of the Council is, whilst in office, a Justice of the Peace. Their duties are :—The repair of the main roads and highways, sewerage works, paving, public lighting, and removal of nuisances. Bye-laws were made in 1868, regulating the mode of construction of new streets and new buildings, the prevention of nuisances, and management of slaughter houses.

The sewerage works were constructed in 1862 and were designed by Mr. J. W. Penfold, C.E.

The sewage is conveyed by means of a 15-inch stoneware sewer to the tanks situated close to Goswell Spring, near Anstey Mill, where the sewage is treated by chemical reagents, the effluent being conveyed into the river Wey ; but works for the irrigation of land with the sewage are in contemplation.

The whole of the footways in the Town were formerly paved with flints (called pitchings), but were repaved in

1867, the material employed being the "blue Staffordshire bricks" (so called in the trade) though these were made at Bishop's Waltham. The bricks are laid in what is termed "Herring-bone" fashion, so that in walking the foot is placed upon three bricks at once.

WATER WORKS.

The Water Works are situated on the top of Windmill Hill, and were started in the year 1876. They consist of an engine house, two sets of pumps, a reservoir and engineer's dwelling house. The well was sunk in the chalk to the depth of 135 feet. In 1880, the supply of water not proving sufficient, the well had to be lowered, but owing to the difficulties encountered, it was only carried a few feet. Boring operations were then instituted and reached a depth of nearly 400 feet. The total depth of the well from the surface is 547 feet. Since this date a plentiful supply of water has been mainained. The Town is well supplied and hydrants are placed at intervals along the mains.

Water Works. 1876.

INFECTIOUS HOSPITAL.

An old building in Cutpound was altered and adapted for the purpose of an Infectious Hospital, and opened in the year 1893. It consists of two large airy wards, kitchen, and good bath arrangements, and will accommodate eight patients. It has proved a great boon to the Town.

Infectious Hospital. 1893.

RECREATION GROUND.

The Alton Recreation and Sports Ground is situated at Anstey, next to Eggar's Grammar School. It was started by the formation of a Company in the year 1890. It is used for recreation, cricket, football, tennis, fêtes, and general out-door amusements.

Recreation Ground. 1890.

The only available ground for such purposes before was the Alton Butts, the large open green at the south-west end of the Town on the Chawton Road, which was public and unenclosed.

PHOTO-ENGRAVING WORKS.

Messrs Vaus and Crampton's Photo-Engraving Works, London and Alton, were started at Beech, near Alton, in March, 1894. The light and air was found to be specially good and suitable for the work.

The picture is photographed and transferred to the copper or zinc plates, which are then engraved by means of acid. The plates can be completed by this process in a few hours; and are used for illustrating books, magazines, etc. As many as twenty-five hands are employed at the present time.

CONSTITUTIONAL CLUB.

This Club, situated in a building belonging to Mr. Cox, in the Market Square, was started in the year 1893.

FRIENDLY SOCIETIES.

The old benefit societies that were founded upon a sharing basis, such as the Duke's Head Club, the King's Head Club (with its white smock frocks) and others, have all died out.

The Modern Order of Foresters began in 1850, but was never registered.

The Registered Friendly Societies, large affiliated Societies, based upon sound principles, are now the recognised benefit clubs, such as " The Hampshire Friendly Society," that started in the year 1825 ; " The Independent Order of Oddfellows," that commenced its career with a very imposing procession in the year 1844 ; and " The Ancient Order of Foresters," in 1869. These Societies are all in a flourishing condition.

The Hampshire Friendly Society numbers now (1895) 550 members.

The Independent Order of Oddfellows, No. 2307, numbers 268 members, and the funds of the Lodge amount to about £4150.

The Ancient Order of Foresters, No. 5373, numbers 313 members, and the funds of the Lodge are about £2049.

LOCAL CELEBRITIES.

Alton itself cannot boast of many distinguished sons, but mention may be made of the following :—

"The Town of Alton gave name to William de Alton, 1307. a Dominican Friar, who wrote in King Edward II's reign. He was the author of a work entitled, *The Universality of the Pollution of Mankind by Original Sin.*"[1]

"Another writer named John Pitts, or Friar Pitts, was 1560. born in Alton in the year 1560, and educated at Winchester. He wrote a book called, *De Illustribus Angliæ Scriptoribus*, which contained an account of all the famous English and Scottish writers up to that period. Pitts became a distinguished scholar and dignitary of the Church of Rome, and died Dean of Verdun, in Lorraine, 1616."[1]

Edmund Spencer, the Poet, it appears resided for a time in Alton and it is supposed lived in a house with a gabled front in Amery street, the old house now next door to the Salvation Barracks. The following extract is taken from the *Life of Edmund Spencer* :—

"A degree of doubt rests on the exact date of his return to Ireland, some asserting that it was in 1591, and others in 1592 ; some that he remained in England till he had 1592. superintended the publication of *The Tears of the Muses*, residing a portion of the time in Alton, Hampshire, and writing there *The Ruins of Time*, while others think that he departed after collecting the materials of the volume and leaving them with Ponsonby."[2]

"William Pinnock, the author of the well-known series of School Books. His father was a labourer in the Town. He, being clever at his books, became an usher at the Grammar School, the Headmaster being the Rev. James Duncan. He afterwards set up as a printer and stationer, probably on the spot where Mr. Hetherington's shop now stands. He was afterwards in business at Winchester and Newbury, then in London, where he died."[3]

---

[1] Extract from *Magna Britanniæ et Hiberniæ*, 1720.
[2] *Life of Edmund Spencer*, by the Rev. George Gilfillan, p. 19.
[3] Extracts from a Lecture, by Rev. John Vaughan.

John Henry Newman was also connected with this
Town. Seventy years ago, when the venerable Cardinal
was an undergraduate at Oxford, he was accustomed to
spend some of his vacations at Alton. A relation of his
(whether father or uncle is uncertain) had some connection
with the brewery now owned by Mr. Hall. He lived in
the house in the High Street, now known as Swarthmore,
and here it was that J. H. Newman used to pass his
holidays. An aunt of mine, an old lady, still living, can
remember seeing Newman standing on the door step of his
house and calling his dog. In a letter written by him to
Canon Durst on the subject of his residence in Alton, he
says : " I was born and lived in London till I got my
Fellowship at Oriel. During a portion of my undergraduate career I was at Alton for the vacation. I never
knew the place in any other way, but I have a pleasant
recollection of beautiful walks and rides about it, and of
the fine hop gardens."

1746.   William Curtis, the distinguished Botanist, and the author
of the *Flora Londinensis* and of the *Botanical Magazine*, was
born in Alton, in the year 1746, in the house in Lenton Street,
now occupied by Mr. Burrell. His father, John Curtis, was
a Tanner. He first commenced his school life at Holybourne, and afterwards went to Burford, in Oxfordshire.
As a boy he early evinced a love for natural history, and
would spend all his pocket money in buying botanical
books. Among the friends of his boyhood was a man
named Legg, who though in humble circumstances (he was
ostler at the Crown) had a great knowledge of local plants
and insects. With this well chosen friend he would spend
his holidays in rambling over the country round Alton.
His father, like a wise man, seeing the bent of his son's
mind, made him a doctor. He was apprenticed to his
grandfather, John Curtis, an apothecary, on Normandy
Hill. He only remained in medical practice for a time,
and retired from it, so as to devote his whole time to
botanical studies. He was appointed Demonstrator of
Plants to the Company of Apothecaries, and established a

WILLIAM CURTIS THE BOTANIST.
1800.

Plate XXI.

botanical garden, arranged for purposes of study. This garden, the first known in England, was originally in Lambeth Marsh, but was afterwards established at Brompton.

Many grasses now in common use were first introduced to agriculturists by Mr. Curtis, and we are indebted to him for that useful vegetable, sea kale.

William Curtis was more than a successful gardener, for he has left two great and valuable works behind him, the *Flora Londinensis* and the *Botanical Magazine.*

He died suddenly at the early age of 53, in the year 1799, and was buried in Battersea Churchyard, and on his tomb-stone is written :—

> " While common herbs shall spring profusely wild,
>   Or garden cherish all that's blithe and gay,
>   So long thy works shall praise dear Nature's child,
>   So long thy memory suffer no decay."

Turning to the celebrities of the immediate neighbour- 1588. hood, the name of George Wither, the Poet, is the first to be mentioned.

He was born at Bentworth in the year 1588. His father was in good circumstances and owned an estate there. He was educated at Magdalen College, Oxford, but on his father's death he returned to Bentworth. We next find him reading at Lincoln's Inn. In 1613, Withers being twenty-five years old, published a satirical poem, entitled " Abuses—Shipt and Whipt," in which are seven allusions to the Beeches at Bentworth, for which he was rewarded by imprisonment in the Marshalsea. On the outbreak of the Civil War between Charles and the Parliament, Wither, who was an ardent politician, threw himself with enthusiasm into the cause of liberty, and even sold his property at Bentworth, or part of it, in order to raise a troop of horse for the Parliament. He became a Major in Cromwell's army and published a poem called *The Protector.* Wither lived to be an old man and was residing in London at the time of the Great Fire. His writings, which are voluminous, are now little known. One of his songs is famous, the first verse being :—

M

> "Shall I, wasting in despair,
> Die, because a woman's fair?
> Or make pale my cheeks with care,
> Cause another's rosie are!
>> Be she fairer than the day,
>> Or the flowery meads in May,
>> If she think not well of me,
>> What care I how fair she be"?

1720. The distinguished Naturalist, Gilbert White, was born at Selborne on 18 July, 1720. He was educated at Basingstoke, and at the age of nineteen went up to the University at Oxford. He was a few years later elected to a Fellowship at Oriel and took holy orders. The last forty years of his life he spent at Selborne, inheriting the Wakes from his uncle. He died at the age of 73 on 26th June, 1793. He left behind him his *History of Selborne.*

Jane Austen was born at Steventon Vicarage, near Basingstoke. Her brother Edward, having inherited from a distant cousin the estate of Chawton House, on which he took the name of Knight, offered his Mother and Sister a home in the Village, and they removed to Chawton in the
1809. year 1809.

The house she lived in is the one now used as "The Workmen's Improvement Club." She wrote many works, some of the best known being " Pride and Prejudice," "Mansfield Park," "Emma" and "Persuasion." She died at Winchester at the early age of 41, on 13th July, 1817, and lies buried in Winchester Cathedral.

Alton is mentioned in Thackeray's *Vanity Fair.*

"Mr. Joseph Sedley is represented as journeying from Southampton to London in a post-chaise. After having partaken of a copious breakfast, with fish, rice and hard eggs at Southampton, he had so far rallied at Winchester as to think a glass of sherry necessary. At Alton he stepped out of his carriage, at his servant's request and imbibed some of the ale for which the place is famous."

This is supposed to have occurred about the year 1827.

The adventure of Prince Edward with the Outlaw of Alton Wood, Adam Gurdon, is made the commencement of the tale in the book entitled *The Prince and the Page*, by the Author of *The Heir of Redclyffe.*

In Shakspere's Play of King Henry VI, Part I, Act iv, Scene vii, the following occurs :—

[*Sir William Lucy after the battle is conducted to the Dauphin's tent, to know what prisoners had been taken and to survey the bodies of the dead.*]

" *Lucy.*—But where's the great Alcides of the field,
Valiant Lord Talbot, earl of Shrewsbury ?
Created for his rare success in arms,
Great earl of Washford, Waterford and Valence ;
Lord Talbot of Goodrig and Urchinfield,
Lord Strange of Blackmere, Lord Verdun of Alton," etc.

SEVERE TEMPEST IN ALTON.

The following account of a tremendous tempest that occurred at Alton on 19th December, 1686, is taken from a tract, printed on folio paper, by Randall Taylor, near Stationers Hall. It consists of a title page and one other page only :—

"STRANGE AND TERRIBLE NEWS FROM

ALTON IN HAMPSHIRE

BEING A FULL AND TRUE ACCOUNT

OF A

DREADFUL TEMPEST

WHICH HAPPENED THERE BY

THUNDER AND LIGHTNING

DECEMBER 19TH, 1686.

Tempest. 1686.

"Amongst all those Varieties of Natural Accidents that either cause our Fear or occasion our Amazement, there is certainly nothing that more contributes to both of them than Thunder and Lightning: In the rest of the methods that the Almighty pleases to evidence His Power to the World, these are more manifest signs of His mercy and mildness than His Anger and Displeasure, as the Reader may find in the following Relation.

"On the nineteenth of December, 1686, at Alton in Hampshire there happened such a Tempest that for the strangeness of its circumstances can scarce be parallel'd in any History ; whether we consider the violence of the Storm, or its duration, or the favourable Exit it made.

"On Sunday when the Reverend Minister of the Parish was towards the latter end of his Prayer before Sermon, it grew on a sudden so exceeding dark that the People could hardly discern one another, and immediately after happened such flashes of lightning that the whole Church seemed to be in a bright flame ; the surprise of the Congregation was exceeding great, especially when two Balls of Fire that made their entry at the Eastern Wall, pass'd through the body of the Church, leaving behind 'em so great a Smoke, and Smell of Brimstone as is scarce able to be expresst. The people endeavoured all they could to get out of the Church, and as it generally happens in such occasions, the Throng and Pressing at the Door was so great and tumultuous, that it was a considerable time before they got out ; some of them fainted away in the Church, as namely the Clerk, who, when he came to himself, cry'd out, Good People where be yee ; some swounded in the Churchyard, and others in their own houses, so great an impression had the Tempest made on them, In short, both within and without, the cry of Women and Children was exceeding affrightful ; but to the everlasting remembrance of so strange an event none were killed, Lightning and Thunder cannot go a hairs breadth beyond the Almighties Commission ; Winds and Tempests fulfil His Words.

"Thus for the Relation of the Tempest in General ; come we now to the particular Damages it wrought ; it broke a hole through the Tower about the bigness of a Cannon-Bullet-hole, and went away by the brim of the great Bell ; it melted above sixty foot of Wire, and passing down into the Clock-room, removed several Boards, and threw a Stone from off the top of a Pillar down among the People, making at the same time as great a noise as the largest Piece of Ordnance in England. It has shatter'd and broke the Windows all round the Church, and likewise a very substantial strong Door that goes into the Tower. Also it came in at a Door upon the Leads, shaking down a great part of the Wall and setting (as 'tis supposed) the middle Loft on Fire, which by the timely care of the People was immediately quench'd and suppressed. The Weather-Cock was carried quite away, and the hand and Boards belonging to the Clock fell among the Congregation. Several Houses in Alton were extremly shook with the

violence of the Storm, that the People ran out of Doors, fearing
their Houses would fall upon their Heads. William Hamman a
Shoemaker had his Head broke, as likewise Joseph Esments.
The Minister (whose name is Mr. Henry Butler, and who justifies
the truth of the whole Relation) had his Eye-brows singed with the
lightning; his Eyes were extreamly sore by the burning that happened; as several others of the Parish, that shared with him in
this unfortunate Accident. The Wall behind the Pulpit has
suffered much Damage; the Steeple was set on Fire, which was
soon extinguished by the Industry of the Townsmen. To give
you the words of a Gentleman who had the Curiosity to go and
view the Ruins some few daies afterwards; I never in my life
(saies he) saw a Sight so dreadful and amazing; and found my
self extreamly concern'd to see the Walls (some whereof are six
or eight Foot wide and square) shatter'd and rent after such a
dismal manner; I touched the Wall about the Breach, and the
Stones crumbled under my Fingers. The Thunder Clap put the
People in such a Consternation, that few of them were able to give
a satisfactory account of the matter etc.

"To conclude, as we have great reason to admire the infinite
goodness and mercy of the Lord upon this occasion; (not one
single person being killed, tho some were wounded) so we ought
to apply the case home to our selves, and by a timely quitting our
sinful courses, avert those Judgments that otherwise will unavoid-
ably fall upon us. Some of our Neighbouring Nations (as the
Gazette has inform'd us) have sufficiently smarted under Heavens
displeasure. The better part of Friezeland lies covered with the
water: whole Villages and Towns swept away by the Deluge; and
some parts of the Castle of St. Angelo at Rome carried by the
force of the Inundation. Let Atheists and Hipocrites beware in
time, and return to the performance of those Duties, which they
are obliged to do as men, and as Christians: For those that will
not listen to the Voice of the Lord in His Scriptures, shall hear,
against their Wills, His Voice in Thunder, and those that are not
to be reduced by the Almighties Clemency, must be reclaimed by
a Judgement.

"Witnessed by
William Hamman.
John Deane.
William Constance, Sexton."

GEOLOGY OF TOWN AND NEIGHBOURHOOD.[1]

The Alton district is situated upon the edge of the chalk formation, and several other strata cropping out from beneath it, will explain the diversified aspect of the country and the variety of soils to be met with in a tract of comparatively limited extent.

The Town of Alton is situated on the lower chalk in the valley of the River Wey, a small stream rising within the parish and running under the street nearly at right angles to it. Alton is nearly surrounded by hills. Towards the north and west the upper chalk attains a considerable elevation. Towards the north-west is a winding valley followed by the road to Basingstoke, in which the Wey rises, and in the south-westerly direction is a broader valley containing the villages of Chawton, Farringdon and East Tisted, on the road to Gosport. Immediately to the south-east of the Town is a hill of lower chalk which turns the river more towards the north, and on the other side of the hill is a narrow valley excavated in the upper marly beds of the green sand formation, which after heavy rains gives passage to a large body of water from Chawton and Farringdon, which flows past Truncheaunts and Caker, and is received into the Wey a little eastward of the Town, at Lynch Hill just beyond Anstey Mill, and passing on in a north-easterly direction, follows the valley along which the London Road is carried. At Froyle the river breaks through the malm rock, and then passes over the gault towards Farnham.

Besides Alton the parishes of Newton, Farringdon, Chawton, Holybourne, and the greater part of Froyle are upon the lower chalk, extending about eight miles nearly in a line from north-east to south-west. From Newton the chalk advances considerably towards the east and south, forming the celebrated Selborne Hill, Nore Hill (a bold promontory) and a line of steep slopes covered with wood, called " Hangers," extending in the direction of Petersfield,

---

[1] *Sketch of the Geology of the Town and Neighbourhood.* Written by my father, William Curtis.

and forming a most picturesque tract of country. At the latter place the lofty range of the South Downs commences.

Eastward of the river from Farringdon to Froyle, the Green Sand formation rises with a gradual slope, following in many instances very nearly the plane of stratification, and extends into the parishes of Selborne, Hartley, East and West Worldham, and Binstead. The Malm Rock, the principal member of the Upper Green Sand formation in this district, attains in the above parishes a considerable elevation, and then terminates abruptly, forming a bold escarpment, covered with beautiful sloping woods or " Hangers." Hartley Hanger and Temple Hanger, spoken of by Gilbert White, are thus formed.

At the base of the escarpment of the Malm Rock occurs the gault which at Bentley and Binsted has its greatest development. In the latter parish the Alice Holt forest stands upon it, and here the elevation of the gault is nearly equal to that of any of the neighbouring strata, an unusual circumstance I believe with that bed. In the rest of its course it forms only a narrow band between the Malm Rock terrace and the Lower Green Sand, which extends several miles towards the east.

The Lower Green Sand is here a highly ferruginous bed, analagous to that of Shanklin. Upon it the parish of Kingsley is situated and a part of Selborne.

Towards the south-west and west are the remaining parishes situated on the upper chalk, namely, East Tisted, Medsted, Bentworth, Lasham, and Shalden.

In the Curtis Museum will be found a very complete collection of the Local Geology, collected by my late father.

Case 26.—1st.

In this case will be found Fossils in Flint from the gravel beds of Alton and the neighbourhood. Fragments of the grinding teeth and bones of the fossil elephant, Millcourt ; horn of the red deer, Noar Hill, 1877 ; and rounded fragments of Greenstone, Farringdon, from the gravel or drift.

Case 27.—2nd.

Tertiary Clay and Sand with numerous Flints, containing fossil sponges, sea urchins and bivalve shells, from Thedden, Shalden, Chawton and Selborne.

Case 28.—3rd.

Upper Chalk (chalk with flints). Flint and Chalk fossils, as sponges, sea urchins, bivalves, terebratulæ, etc. Alton, Great Wood, Shalden, Medsted, West Tisted, Holybourne.

Case 29.—4th.

Lower Chalk (chalk without flints) and Grey Chalk, sea urchins and their spines, bivalve shells, terebratulæ, ammonites, nautilites, belemnites, bones, palatal teeth and scales of fish, and tooth of lizard. Alton, Wilsham, Caker Hill, Neatham, Selborne, etc. One ammonite in this case exhibits its syphon.

Cases 29 and 30.—5th.

Chalk Marl. Numerous fossils, differing in different localities, and therefore arranged according to the places where they occur. Amongst these is an interesting collection of the shells of the cephalopoda or cuttles, namely, nautilus, ammonites, and turrilites. One specimen, turrilites tuberculates, found at Neatham, exhibits its syphon, seen as a black line following two of the whorls of the shell, which only one other specimen, in the British Museum is known to do. Localities—Caker Hill, Wilsham, Monk Wood, Lynch Hill, Neatham, West Worldham road, Selborne and Hawkley.

Case 31.—6th.

Chloritic, or Green Sand, the upper bed of the Upper Green Sand, containing Ammonites, inoceramus, ventrilites, pectens, tooth of shark, etc. Localities—Neatham, Selborne.

Case 31.—7th.

Malm Rock, or Fire Stone, the chief member of the Upper Green Sand in this district. Numerous fossils, beginning with a few minerals, namely, pure allumina, crystallized carbonate of lime, and quartz or rock crystal. A few vegetable remains. Sea urchins and a unique specimen of star fish. Bivalve shells and a few univalves. Shells of the cephalopoda or cuttle fishes, namely, hamites (hamus, a hook, from their shape), ammonites, belemnites, nautilites, etc. Localities—Millcourt, Quarley Bottom, Froyle, Binsted, Selborne.

Case 32.

Amongst these may be particularly noticed ammonites, with the keel terminating in a spine or beak, and a few specimens of nautilus, containing crystallized quartz in their inner chambers. Also a few remains of crabs, teeth of reptiles and sharks, fish scales, etc., and collection of fossils from the Gault, the bed of blue clay which separates the Upper from the Lower Green Sand. Most of them were obtained from the first railway cutting, made in 1847, just beyond the present Bentley Station. The remainder of this case is filled with the rocks and fossils of the Lower Green Sand (in this locality a ferruginous or iron sand) from Kingsley, Headley, etc.

The remainder of the local larger fossils will be found in the top shelf of Cases 20, 21 and 22 ; and on the floor, boulders from the drift, etc., some large ammonites from the local chalk of Borovere, Wilsham, Lower Froyle, etc., and flints and Malm rock specimens.

BRITISH BIRDS.

There is a very fine collection of Birds to be seen in the Curtis Museum, but I only intend enumerating those found in Alton and its neighbourhood.

ORDER I.—RAPTORES (BIRDS OF PREY).

Osprey—killed at Lasham or Herriard. Presented to the Museum 1858. Very rare.

Peregrine Falcon—Froyle, 1863, Alton. Very rare.

Hobby—Alton. A rare summer migrant.

Merlin—a rare winter visitant. One killed at Neatham Mill, August 1889.

Kestrel—Alton. Common.

Sparrow Hawk—Alton.

Common Buzzard—Hackwood. Occasionally seen in the neighbourhood. (A Rough-Legged Buzzard was shot at Froyle in March, 1895.)

Hen Harrier—Hackwood. Very rare. (One killed near Wolmer Pond, Autumn, 1893.)

Montagu's Harrier—Newton. Very rare.

Barn Owl—Alton.

Long-Eared Owl—Alton and Lasham.

Short Eared Owl—Alton and Medstead.   Autumnal migrant to
England.

Tawny Owl—Alton.

ORDER II.—INSESSORES (PERCHING BIRDS).

Red-backed Shrike—Alton.   A summer migrant.

Missel Thrush—Alton.

Song Thrush—Alton.   One albino specimen.

Fieldfare—Alton.   A winter visitant.

Redwing—Alton.   A winter visitant.

Blackbird—Alton.

Ring Ouzel—Alton.   A spring and autumn migrant to south of
England.

Hedge Sparrow—Alton.

Redbreast—Alton.

Redstart—Alton.   A summer migrant.

Black Redstart—King's Pond, Alton, 1865.   A rare winter
visitant.

Stonechat—Alton.

Winchat—Alton.   A summer migrant.

Wheatear—Alton.   A summer migrant.

Nightingale—Alton.   A summer migrant.

Blackcap—Alton.   A summer migrant.

Dartford Warbler—Wolmer Forest, 1847.   Rare.

Willow Wren—Alton ; a summer migrant.   Common.

Golden Crested Wren—Alton.

Common Wren—Alton.

Tree Creeper—Alton.   Not uncommon.

Nuthatch—Alton.

Great Titmouse—Alton.

Blue Titmouse—Alton.

Long-tailed Titmouse—Alton.   Not uncommon.

Waxwing—Alton.   A rare irregular winter visitant.

Pied Wagtail—Alton.

Grey Wagtail—Alton.   Chiefly a winter visitant.

Rays or Yellow Wagtail—Alton.   A summer migrant.

Meadow Pipit—Alton.

Sky Lark—Alton.

Common Bunting—Alton.

Reed, or Black-headed Bunting—Alton.

Yellow Bunting, or Yellow Ammer—Alton.
Cirl Bunting—Alton. Uncommon.
Chaffinch—Alton.
Brambling—Alton. A winter visitant.
Goldfinch—Alton.
Siskin—Alton. An occasional winter visitant.
Mealy Redpole—Alton. An occasional winter visitant.
Tree Sparrow—Alton.
House Sparrow—Alton.
Greenfinch—Alton.
Hawfinch—Midhurst. Occasionally seen in this district.
Bullfinch—Alton.
Crossbill—Alton, 1878. Four specimens. A rare spring and
    autumn migrant.
Starling—Alton.
Raven—two from Hackwood. Now very rare in England.
Carrion Crow—Alton.
Hooded Crow—Alton. Winter visitant in south of England.
Rook—Alton.
Jackdaw—Alton.
Magpie—Alton.
Jay—Alton.
Green Woodpecker—Alton. Not uncommon.
Greater Spotted Woodpecker—Alton, 1859. Rare. (One shot
    in Great Wood, Spring, 1894, and a female and two young
    at Bentworth, July, 1895.)
Lesser Spotted Woodpecker—Millcourt. Rare.
Wryneck—Alton. Summer migrant.
Cuckoo and young Cuckoo—Alton. A summer migrant.
Kingfisher—Alton.
Swallow—Alton. A summer migrant.
Martin—Alton. A summer migrant.
Swift—Alton. A summer migrant.
Nightjar—Alton. A summer migrant.

ORDER III.—RASORES (SCRAPERS).

Ring Dove—Alton.
Stock Dove—Alton.
Turtle Dove...Alton. A summer migrant.
Pheasant—Alton.
Partridge, and case with young—Alton.

Red-Legged Partridge — Alton. (Introduced into England about 1770.)

Quail—Alton. One killed at Alton, Autumn, 1890.

ORDER IV.—GRALLATORES (WADING BIRDS).

Stone Curlew—Alton. A summer migrant. Breeds in this neighbourhood.

Golden Plover—Alton. A winter visitant to south of England.

Lapwing and young—Alton.

Ringed Plover—Alton, 1858.

Greenshank—Oakhanger, 1861. Wolmer Forest, 1862.

Spotted Redshank (in case)—Selborne. Presented by Professor Bell. Very rare.

Green Sandpiper—Selborne, 27 August, 1859.

Ruff and Reeve (male without ruff).—King's Pond, Alton.

Common Sandpiper—Hawkley, 1855.

Grey Phalarope—Selborne, 1867. Alton. An autumn migrant.

Woodcock—Alton. Occasionally breeds in England.

Common Snipe—Alton. Breeds at Shortheath.

Jack Snipe—Alton. A winter visitant.

Heron and Young—Alton.

Water Rail—Alton.

Land Rail—Alton. A summer migrant.

Moorhen—Alton.

Coot—Alton.

ORDER V.—NATATORES (WEBB-FOOTED BIRDS).

Brent Goose (in case). Winter Visitant.

Egyptian Goose—King's Pond, Alton. Winter Visitant.

White-fronted Goose—Alton. Winter Visitant.

Wild Duck—Alton.

Widgeon—Alton.

Teal—Alton. Breeds in Wolmer Forest.

Scaup—King's Pond, Alton. A winter visitant.

Tufted Duck—Alton. A winter visitant.

Red-breasted Merganser—King's Pond, Alton. A winter visitant to England.

Goosander—Millcourt, Alton. A winter visitant to England.

Great Northern Diver—Medstead, 1866. A winter visitant to England.

Red-throated Diver. (Shot at Newton Valence, Autumn, 1893.)

Little Grebe, or Dabchick—Alton.

Puffin. (Caught at Froyle, November, 1892).

Razor-Bill—Alton. (One caught on Neatham Down, Autumn, 1893.)

Guillemot—Alton, January, 1887.

Little Auk—Wield, Alton. January, 1895.

Common Tern—King's Pond, Alton, 10 October, 1857, and Hartley.

Black Tern—Hartley, Alton.

Kittiwake—Alton.

Common Gull—Alton.

To make the collection of British Birds more complete, specimens have been added from other parts of England and Scotland.

LOCAL QUADRUPEDS.

ORDER CHEIROPTERA. (HAND-WINGED) BATS.

The Great Bat.

The Long-eared Bat.

The Common Bat or Flitter-mouse.

ORDER INSECTIVORA. (INSECT EATERS.)

The Hedgehog, with young.

The Mole—specimens of various colours, and young.

The Common Shrew.

ORDER CARNIVORA. (FLESH EATERS.)

The Badger—three adult specimens, one of which is an Albino, and one young one.

The Otter—two specimens.

The Weasel—one male and three females. The female is much smaller than the male, and known as a " Crane " or " Cane " in this district.

The Stoat or Ermine Weasel—four specimens, two in summer, and two in winter dress.

The Polecat, or Fitchet Weasel—Monk Wood. Now almost extinct in the South of England.

The Common Marten—Hackwood. Extinct in England.

The Fox—male and female, and young.

The Squirrel—three specimens.

Dormouse.

Harvest Mouse.

Long-tailed Field Mouse.

Common Mouse.

Brown or Common Rat—three specimens, one parti-coloured, and one young ; two Albinos with red eyes.

Water-Vole, or Water Rat.   Feeds chiefly on plants.

Common Field Vole.

Hare and Leveret, and one Hybrid.

Rabbit, and one Albino specimen.

THE FLORA OF ALTON.[1]

The district around Alton, as the varied nature of the soil would lead us to expect, is peculiarly rich in wild flowers.   The extensive woodlands, the chalk hills, the beech hangers, the valley of the Wey, the bogs of Wolmer Forest, with its wide stretches of uncultivated moorland, the hollow lanes towards Selborne, even the hedge-banks and wastes beside the roads, all yield their own individual Flora. The Alton district is also of quite exceptional interest, owing to the neighbourhood of Selborne, which is classic ground to all true naturalists.   White's forty-first letter to Daines Barrington gives a short list of the rarer plants of Selborne and Wolmer Forest, and the pleasure of comparing the Flora of the neighbourhood as given by the great naturalist one hundred years ago with the Flora of to-day can hardly be exaggerated.   Many of the plants mentioned by White still flourish in their old localities : both the long-leaved (*D. intermedia*) and the round-leaved Sundew may be found in " the bogs of Bin's Pond," but the marsh cinque-foil (*Comarum palustre*, L.) has not been seen there of late years.   The golden Saxifrage (*Chrysosplenium Oppositifolium*, L.) still grows " in the dark and rocky

By the Rev. John Vaughan, M.A., Vicar of Portchester, and formerly Curate of Alton.

hollow lanes," and the "Spurge laurel" on Selborne Hanger, but the *Daphne Mezereum*, L., has, I fear, disappeared.

I do not propose to give a complete list of the plants of the neighbourhood, but rather to mention the rarer and more interesting ones. Neither shall I be too definite as to the exact "habitat" of the choicer plants, lest, as might possibly happen, those plants should disappear. Let me add that no true botanist will ever endanger the existence of the rarer species, but on the contrary will use every endeavour to preserve them.

The following species may be included in the Flora of Alton and of the Alton district, within a radius of five miles :—

Helleborus fœtidus, L. Stinking Hellebore or Setterwort. Rare and becoming rarer.

H. Viridis, L. Green Hellebore. In one or two localities in fair abundance. Still to be found in White's locality.

Erysimum Cheiranthoides, L. Occasionally in Wolmer Forest. I found it in 1885 and 1887.

Nasturtium palustre, D.C. Shortheath.

Arabis perfoliata, Lam. Very rare. One spot only.

Teesdalia nudicaulis, Br. Abundant in the Forest and on Shortheath.

Viola palustris, L. Bins Pond and Forest bogs.

Saponaria officinalis, L. Occasionally.

Astragalus glycyphyllus, L. One locality only.

Lathyrus Nissolia, L. Very rare.

L. Sylvestris, L. In several localities, including Gilbert White's.

Potentilla argentea, L. One locality only.

Geum rivale, L. Very rare in this district.

Sedum Telephium, L. Copses and Hangers.

Dipsacus pilosus, L. Not uncommon in small copses and by the wayside, as at Chawton.

Gnaphalium Sylvaticum, L. Chawton Park, Ackender and other woods. Not uncommon.

Erigeron acris, L. Plentiful on the Chalk hills, such as Holybourne Down.

Vaccinium Oxycoccus, L. Cranberry. Shortheath, where it grew in White's time.

Pyrola minor, L. This interesting plant may still be found in
    this parish.

Monotropa Hypopithys, L. Selborne, Chawton.

Chlora perfoliata, L. Not common.

Gentiana Amarella, L. Common on the Chalk hills.

Menyanthes trifoliata, L. Rare.

Atropa Belladonna, L. Deadly Nightshade. In one or two
    localities.

Hyoscyamus niger, L. Henbane. Occasionally in gardens and
    waste places.

Linaria Elatine, Mill. Uncommon.

L. repens, Mill. Sanfoil field at Alton in 1892.

Lathræa Squamaria, L. In one or two copses in the neigh-
    bourhood. Not seen lately in White's locality.

Mentha Pulegium, L. Kingsley.

Marrubium Vulgare, L. White Horehound, Shortheath.

Leonurus Cardiaca, L. Motherwort. Shortheath. This is pro-
    bably White's locality, "Forest-side."

Pulmonaria Officinalis, L. Lungwort. This plant grows in one
    copse only in the neighbourhood.

Cynoglossom officinale, L. Hound's tongue. Shortheath. Not
    uncommon.

Polygonum Bistorta, L. Selborne.

P. minus, Huds. Shortheath.

Daphne Mezereum, L. Still growing in one or two woods in
    the neighbourhood. Lost on Selborne Hill.

Euphorbia Cyparissias, L. Shalden; introduced probably with
    young trees.

Orchis pyramidalis, L. In several places.

O. latifolia, L. Marsh Orchis. Wet meadows, Alton.

Habenaria bifolia, Bab. Fairly common.

H. Chlorantha, Bab. Fairly common.

Ophrys apifera, Huds. Bee Orchis, Alton. Some years in
    plenty.

O. Muscifera, Huds. Fly Orchis. In several places, outside
    woods.

Spiranthes autumnalis, Rich. Chalk hills, abundant.

Neottia Nidus-avis, Rich. Bird's Nest Orchis. Not common :
    generally distributed.

Cephalanthera grandiflora, Bab. To be found in many woods.

C. Ensifolia, Rich. This beautiful plant grows in two copses
    in the district.

Epipactus latifolia, Sw. Selborne, Alton, Chawton.

E. media, Bab. Same localities. Not uncommon.

E. purpurata, Sm. This very rare Helleborine is to be found in several places about Alton.

Narcissus Pseudo-Narcissus, L. Daffodil. Worldham Hanger. Abundant.

Galanthus nivalis, L. Snowdrop. In several localities.

Tulipa Sylvestris, L. Wild Tulip. This exceedingly rare and beautiful plant may still be included in our local Flora. I saw it in flower this year, 1894. The Selborne Plants have not blossomed of late years, but the leaves may be found.

Narthecium ossifragum, Huds. Bog Asphodel. Abundant in Wolmer Forest.

Paris quadrifolia, L. Common in the woods throughout the district.

Poligonatum multiflorum, All. Solomon's Seal. Common in the woods and copses.

Scirpus sylvaticus, L. Kingsley. Shortheath.

S. setaceus, L. Kingsley Pond.

Carex curta. Shortheath. Kingsley.

C. bracteata, Syme. Bins Wood.

C. pallescens, L. Chawton Park ; Butler's Copse.

C. ampullacea, Good. Kingsley.

Holcus mollis, L. Alton. Chawton Park.

Triticum caninum, Huds. Ackender.

Hordeum Sylvaticum, Huds. Ackender.

H. pratense, Huds. Alton Old Road.

Asplenium Trichomanes, L. Formerly on the walls of Alton Church, now unfortunately disappeared.

A. Adiantum-nigrum, L. Bentworth.

Athyrium Filix-fœmina. The Lady Fern. Chawton Park.

Lastræa spinulosa, Presl. Chawton Park.

Ophioglossum vulgatum, L. Adder's Tongue. Thedden ; Worldham.

Lycopodium inundatum, L. Marsh Club-moss. Common on Shortheath.

It will be noticed that the district is specially rich in Orchidaceæ, of which no less than twenty species have been found about Alton. The following plants have also been recorded by the late Professor Bell and others as occurring in the district, and should be diligently searched for by the local botanist. I have never been fortunate enough to meet with them in the localities indicated, though it is quite likely that some of them may exist.

Myosurus minimus, L. Mousetail. Hollow lanes. Selborne.
Dianthus Armeria, L. Near Bentley.
Trigonella ornithopodioides, D. C. Kingsley.
Lathyrus Aphaca, L. Selborne, 1866.
Parnassia palustris. Oakhanger.
Bartsia viscosa, L. The Lyth, Selborne.
Mentha Sylvestris, L. Selborne.
Melissa Officinalis, L. Balm. Dorton by the Stream, Selborne.
Nepeta Cataria, L. Northfield, Selborne.
Daphne Mezereum, L. Selborne Hanger.
Allium oleraceum, L. Selborne.
Osmunda regalis, L. Oakhanger.
Botrychium Lunaria, Sm. Selborne.

It would be interesting to know that some of the above species had been re-discovered in their old localities.

JOHN   VAUGHAN.

Portchester, July, 1894.

INDEX.

GENERAL INDEX.

INDEX TO
NAMES OF PERSONS MENTIONED.